KISS AND TELL

SHANNON TWEED

with Julie McCarron
Foreword by Gene Simmons

SIMMONS BOOKS/PHOENIX PRESS
Beverly Hills

Printed in the United States of America
ISBN: 159-777-5177
Library of Congress Cataloging-in-Publication Data Available
Design: Kerry DeAngelis, KL Design
Simmons Books/Phoenix Press
9465 Wilshire Boulevard Suite 315
Beverly Hills, CA 90210
www.genesimmons.com
10 9 8 7 6 5 4 3 2 1

KISS AND TELL

Dedication

I want to dedicate this book first to Gene: the man I was looking for, the father of my beautiful children Nick and Sophie, and the man who keeps me grounded and safe, loved and needed.

To my kids, who accept me and love me in spite of my faults and flaws.

To my mother, Mrs. Louise Tweed—who forgives me for quitting school and sneaking out at night—for sacrificing the best years of her life to give us a better life. For not falling into despair. For keeping it together against insurmountable odds. For doing her absolute best! I love and admire her.

To my sister Tracy for being my best friend. To my niece Emily, just for being Emily.

To my friends, especially Janis Kay, for loving me (even when I'm fat!) and making me laugh.

To Dad, thank you!

To Hef, thanks for the memories.

Love to Kim; Kyla; Lance; Sara; Spencer; Nathan; Tarry; Keith Anders, Cole and Erin; Jeff; Casey; Cheryl; Ted; Jake; and Hunter.

GEORGE HURRELL PORTRAIT.

A Word from Gene Simmons

Suddenly there she was. She was wearing a very revealing corset that just barely kept her beautiful breasts and ravishing figure inside. Just barely. She was standing with her sister a few feet away, looking at me. I was in my silk pajamas at the Playboy Mansion's Midsummer Night's Dream party. It happened to be on the night of my birthday, August 25th, and the event was an invitation-only affair for four hundred guests. The ratio of men to women was one to three (three women for every man). The men had to wear pajamas, the women as little as possible.

I had come there with two Playmates and wasn't really looking to flirt with anyone else—I was busy. Then she walked up to me and looked me over. I must have said something, but she quickly turned and walked off. I was stunned. I found her instantly desirable and quickly forgot that I had come with two other ladies.

She walked by again and I threw her my best lines. My patois had worked many times in the past. Not this time. I watched her walk away again on her stiletto heels. She was as sexy from behind as she was from the front.

I found myself walking aimlessly around and finally settled inside the Mansion. I was looking at a Dali painting on the wall and heard a whistle. It was her. We sat down and started talking. I found myself looking into her eyes and actually having a conversation. I told her about myself. While I was listening to her voice, I felt my manhood stand rigidly erect against my silk pajamas. I didn't dare stand up, although she wanted to go somewhere. We sat and continued to talk until things calmed down.

She invited me to go with her through a secret door to a basement wine cellar. We were there alone. I knew she was "inviting" me. Normally, I would have ravaged her right then and there. On the floor, on the pool table. Anywhere. But I did not. I can't for the life of me figure out why.

I wanted to see her again.

That was 22 years ago. I've been living with her ever since.

I continue to paw at her, and she keeps smacking my hand away. I continue to tell her she is the most desirable woman in the world, because she is. She ignores me. When she was pregnant with Nicholas, all I wanted her to do was stay in bed with me. I found myself continually being aroused by her. When she slept. When she walked by. When she talked.

I was crazy about everything she did.

She, on the other hand, couldn't stand the way I chewed my food and left crumbs all over the place. She hates how I rumple the sheets in our bed. She thinks I talk too much. Outside of home, I'm a very important person. At home, I'm usually in the way. And most shocking is that she doesn't feel any reluctance to ask me to take out the garbage. Me! The God of Thunder. The guy with the lasciviously long tongue! The guy who is adored and desired by millions of fans throughout the world.

While on tour (I'm in a band called KISS) I call her every day. She never asked me to; I do it because I want to. And I usually find myself being cut short by her. She doesn't like to chat. Our calls usually end with her saying, "Well, gotta go. Bye."

She has never asked me where I'm going. She does not play the female "torture" game. She has been in my hotel room (on the few times she would join me on tour) when girls would call in the middle of the night. She would answer the phone, and they would run for the hills.

She does what she wants when she wants to, and doesn't check with anyone to see if it's okay to do it—me included. I usually ask her where she's going and if I can come along. Often, the answer is no. I'm lucky if she lets me tag along to the movies with her. And when we're watching the movie, she will often shush me when I whisper a comment to her.

We have never been married. We have two wonderful kids together: Sophie, who has robbed me of my soul, and Nicholas, who I hope to be like when I grow up.

She is everything I never knew I wanted. She makes me a better man. She gives me more freedom than I want. I love her more today than I did when we first met.

I had been reluctant to say "I love you" too much in the past. It always sounded like bad soap opera dialogue. "Honey" and "sweetheart" seemed to me to be clichés people uttered. I preferred to say what I meant and mean what I said. But every day when Sophie and Nicholas leave for school I find myself yelling after them, "I love you." When Nicholas says something kind to me or when Sophie brings me a piece of toast, I well up with tears. When we watch a movie that centers around a family being reunited with their kids, my eyes fill up in the dark.

That's when she turns to me and says, "You're welcome."

She calls me by many names: *Stinky, Stink, Stink-ola, Pops, Papparoonie, Popo* (which, to her delight, she found means "ass" in Hungarian), *Pappo, Pony, Boney* (I'm sure you can figure that one out), *Boney Maroney, My-Opia, O, Old* (she even wrote a little melody that goes something like "Older than time, older than wine...," etc., that she, her sister and my kids often sing to me), *Olie, Andre* (as in the Giant), and numerous others.

On tour, I'm The Demon. At home, I'm Stinky.

The reason I haven't said her name yet is that she doesn't like it. She doesn't like the sound of her first or last name. She doesn't think she's beautiful. She does not think she is special at all. But the truth is, Shannon Tweed, you are the most beautiful woman in the world.

Can I go to the movies with you???

Introduction

I was considerably overdressed for my first party at the Playboy Mansion. At the famous annual Midsummer Night's Dream celebration, where required attire for guests consists of pajamas, lingerie, or nothing, I wore a see-through peignoir—very Canadian of me. You know those Canadians: wild in the bedroom, but conservative in public. At least they were back then.

I had spent all day getting ready, freaking out about what I would wear and noticing that a couple of the other girls also preparing for the party were not wearing nearly as much as I was. I got the feeling they knew something I didn't.

💋   💋   💋

It was a hot August day in 1981 when I flew to L.A. I was a 24-year-old (that's 17 American) pasty-white Canadian girl who had no idea what to expect. On the drive to the Playboy Mansion I got out of the car to touch a palm tree. I had never seen a live palm tree before. It looked bizarre and unreal—like an elephant's foot. I'd never experienced such hot weather before, and the sultry summer heat made my clothes stick to me. Or was it nerves?

On my first evening at the Mansion—at the Midsummer Night's Dream party—I was so anxious about the impression I would make, I couldn't truly let loose and enjoy the evening. I felt a little old-fashioned and out of place. It was such a trendy party packed with major stars, and I was...well, I was me. So it's hard to remember all the details of the evening. Suffice it say, I was dazzled—and overdressed.

The Playboy Mansion is an enormous Tudor-style home on six acres behind guarded gates in Holmby Hills, an exclusive L.A. neighborhood. When I first saw the Mansion, its vast grounds were tented for the party, and it looked like a fantasyland. Peacocks strolled the lush grass. Penned up or wandering freely on the grounds were monkeys, flamingos and all kinds of rare or wild animals. Colorful and exotic birds flew freely in an aviary. The ponds scattered over the grounds were stocked with koi fish. Bunnies and rabbits were everywhere. I had never attended a party of this magnitude. It was a mini-zoo—in more ways than one. And I had never seen a more beautiful, twinkling sight in my life.

There were hundreds of scantily-clad girls everywhere: tall girls, short girls, curvy girls, skinny girls, exotic girls, Asian girls, and African-American girls. I had never seen perfect done in so many ways. They had beauty in common, and they all seemed so uninhibited and relaxed. I had modeled lingerie in catalogs and newspaper ads at home in Canada, but I'd certainly never worn it out in public. (Remember, this was pre-Madonna.) It's a completely different ball game when you're walking around in person, jiggling while people watch. It was not like being photographed for still shots, where I felt a small sense of control over my image and unflattering pictures could be touched up or tossed. Fortunately I was young and didn't have too much jiggle to worry about.

It's well-known among Hollywood insiders that it is virtually impossible for an unknown guy to attend the Midsummer's Night Dream party. Pretty girls were a different story. Even when a Playmate wanted to bring a male friend, it was frowned upon— still is. Naturally there were many of Hugh Hefner's friends in attendance, and most of them were around his age. Hef was in his early fifties at the time—but there were no average Joes at this party. The magical event was held at Hugh Hefner's home, so he had every right to invite whomever he wanted, including a couple of prominent male porn stars (I saw Harry Reems, who was one of the biggest at the time—in more ways than one). A number of major film and television actors were also present. What Hef wanted to do was invite his friends, plus a couple hundred gorgeous girls to keep them happy. The arrangement worked out very well for all involved.

I had to psych myself up to walk into a party of 500 nearly naked people. I was escorted by Playboy public relations representative Elizabeth, which calmed me somewhat. An A-list of actors, comedians, and musicians were all in attendance. That night I met Julie Andrews (Mary Poppins!), and her husband, director

MEETING PAUL NEWMAN!

Blake Edwards, Bill Cosby, Sara Vaughn, Wayne Gretzky, Magic Johnson, Sugar Ray Leonard, Scott Baio, John Belushi, Robin Williams, Helen Gurley Brown, James Caan, Patrick Cassidy, and Wilt Chamberlain, among the partygoers.

I didn't know a single person in the room before I arrived. Well, I knew Paul Newman, but he didn't know me. My first thought on seeing him was that he was shorter than I had pictured. I soon learned that in real life every famous person was shorter than I expected, except for Clint Eastwood, who was larger than life. When you're almost six feet tall, it's hard to be impressed by anyone's height, but I must say Wilt Chamberlain, Kareem Abdul-Jabbar, and Magic Johnson measured up!

I tried not to stare as I was introduced to the entertainers I'd seen all my life in the movies and on television. When we met face-to-face, I was literally looking down on people I considered icons, people I admired and had grown up watching. I was bigger than people who had won Academy Awards, though no one there knew my name. I'm sure I'm never smaller than anyone expects, and I'd later realize that was not always a good thing.

After I scouted around the party a bit, seeing famous faces everywhere I looked, I really needed a couple of stiff drinks. I downed them quickly, just to get the courage to continue making the rounds with Elizabeth, who was introducing me to everyone there as "Miss November 1981, Shannon Tweed from Canada." I wondered if anyone would ever remember my name.

Shortly after I arrived at the party, a man approached me and said, "Hello, I'm Hugh." *Wow, okay, my goodness*, I thought; he was coming on pretty strong, very flirty and touching me. He turned out to be Hugh O'Brien, the actor who played in a lot of old Westerns. I think he did that on purpose—that whole, "Hello, I'm Hugh" thing. I mean, come on, he was there and his name was Hugh and he was wearing pajamas. Naturally I assumed he was Hugh Hefner. I imagine that line worked pretty well for him over the years.

I did eventually meet the real Hugh Hefner that night, the man who would change my life, and believe me, he was so much more charismatic than some TV cowboy. He was the whole package—handsome, brilliant, charming and, most important, very attentive. Half of the attraction for me is that the other person likes you. Why waste time trying to get a man to like you? I never want to work that hard at chemistry. For Hef and me it was there, and it

showed. We were immediately enamored.

The two of us started talking and never really stopped. I had to wonder what he saw in me, a small-town dork. I certainly wasn't a worldly L.A. girl. But overall I felt I was making a good impression; he didn't leave my side for quite some time. His longtime girlfriend, Sondra, was floating around, and she too was very warm and welcoming. I liked them both very much. I liked everything about the Mansion. I envied Sondra living there, and I dreaded having to fly home to my small apartment, cheap car and waitressing jobs.

I stayed for a few days after the party in a guesthouse where girls stayed when they were visiting L.A. or shooting for the magazine. The morning—or should I say afternoon—after the party I walked over to the main mansion for breakfast and sat down in what was called the Mediterranean Room. A butler came out to take my order—certainly my first experience with household help on that level. I had been thinking I would pop into the kitchen and make some toast, though I was a bit nervous about going into somebody else's kitchen, but the other girls steered me to the dining room, where I was free to order whatever I wanted.

I had never tried an avocado before, and bagels were not my usual fare, as Canadians were big on English muffins and toast, so I ordered a toasted bagel with bacon, lettuce, tomato, cream cheese, avocado, and sprouts. I thought it was quite sophisticated and Californian of me to try all of these new things in one sandwich. It was delicious, I loved it, and it would soon become my regular breakfast while in residence.

A new lifestyle was opening up before my eyes. As a fair-skinned girl I had never been a sun worshipper, and I had never intentionally been out in weather this hot, so I had to be extra careful. There were a couple of summers when I'd visited my grandparents' cabin at Emma Lake in Saskatchewan, where I'd burned and freckled and peeled, but that was it for the sun thing. Even though I was almost translucent, I wanted to get with the new program and be a part of L.A. life. I put on my bathing suit and lay out at the pool with a few other girls, trying to do the California thing, and wishing I had those makeup people we used in the bathing suit ads.

Hef usually appeared around midday and stopped by the pool to chat with everyone. He always lingered to talk with me; we had definitely made a connection. Over the next couple of days I saw a little more of what life in the Playboy Mansion was like. There were regular movie screenings, poker and backgammon nights—all kinds of different events where Hef's friends came over to his house and socialized. The Mansion was beautiful, the service was impeccable, and the celebrities were everywhere. They were the most amazing three days of my life. It was life on another planet: Planet Playboy.

I knew what everyone back home was thinking. My family was concerned at what I was getting myself into. My friends were rapidly disappearing—but during my three-day stay I'd already made some new friends. (I'm still close with two of them today. Monique St. Pierre was an exotic beauty with an easy laugh and a beautiful face and body. She had been Playmate of the Year in

1978 and was a regular at Mansion West gatherings. We became close pals and troublemakers during those party days, and had our first-born sons at the same time years later. I met another lifelong friend there, Wendy Leitman, whom I became very close to and still see today, when she's not working as an attorney at Disney or taking care of her twins.) But at the time, all my old friends in Canada were speculating on my actions and criticizing me for taking the "easy way out." I didn't necessarily consider posing for *Playboy* the easy way out, but it was, to say the least, an interesting new path to follow. I wanted a new direction. I had been slinging drinks for six years and was looking for something new. It seemed with *Playboy* my luck was changing. I was up for the ride. I didn't know what doors might open for me, but I knew I was going to turn the handle.

CHAPTER ONE

Mink

A beautiful, pristine Emerald Isle is how I would describe Newfoundland, Canada. It lies at the easternmost point in Canada, northeast of New York, with a similar weather pattern, though a slightly shorter summer.

The farming community of Whitbourne lay just minutes away from our ranch on the coast of Newfoundland. It was the closest thing to a town I ever experienced growing up, but the nearest hospital was in Markland, a few more miles away, so that was where my birth was officially recorded. Whitbourne was where I would

MY MATERNAL GRANDPARENTS

MY MATERNAL GREAT GRANDPARENTS.

MOM AND DAD

attend grade school and receive my very first (disappointing) kiss from a boy, a bass player named Billy.

My parents had seven kids and a mink ranch. We'll get to the kids, but first let me say that mink are the most stinky, smelly animals imaginable. My dad's brother, a fisherman with his own boat, went to the tiny fishing village of Dildo (that's right, you heard it correctly —Dildo) each day. He gave my father any scraps that weren't sold or otherwise used, and my dad threw these together with grains and dead horse parts—pretty much any dead animal part would do. He'd grind all these guts and carcasses together in a meat grinder and feed this mixture to the mink. They thrived on it and bred like... well, like mink.

Mink were killed by breaking their necks, in order to protect the pelt. My dad, his brother, and a couple of ranch hands would go down the rows of pens in the shed... *crack, crack, crack*... a very quick death, really. Then the carcasses were hung upside down by the feet and each fur was carefully cut and peeled off in one piece. The pelts were then skinned of their fat and dried. That was the stinky part.

We raised a few chickens as well, and I can say they actually do run around after their heads are cut off. There was plenty of killing going on at the ranch. Given my upbringing, you'd think I'd be a vegetarian today, but I'm not. It was just farm life. Headless, half-

MOM AND KIM, ANOTHER DOG, ME AND LANCE

dead chickens would race around our yard for thirty seconds or so, wings flapping and blood spurting out of their necks, before finally collapsing in a puff of dirty feathers. My mother would send one of us to retrieve the body before one of the dogs did. Then we would begin the plucking and gutting process—something that involved large pots of steaming hot water and lots of elbow grease. My older

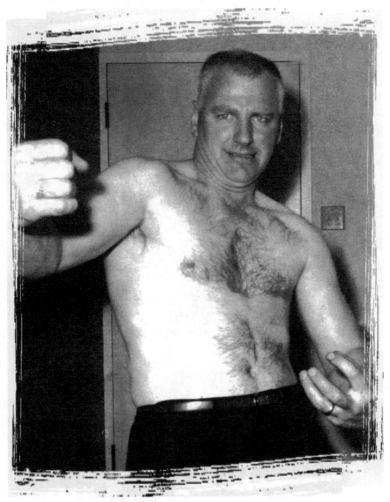

MY DAD – THANK YOU FOR THE EYES, NOSE, LIPS AND MY NEVER-ENDING ACNE.

MOM AND DAD (SMOKING) WITH ME AT 7 MONTHS

brother, Lance, tells me we had other animals, but I don't recall any cows and pigs except for those belonging to the neighbors.

My dad was a big, handsome guy who looked a little like Chris Isaak. He was six-foot-two with a classic V-shape body: wide shoulders, slim waist. He had generous lips and an easy smile; bright blue eyes and large hands. He could snap the neck of a mink with

MA AND PA OUTSIDE THE FIRST HOUSE BEFORE THE FIRE THAT TOOK MOST OF MY BABY PHOTOS. (NOTE THE LOVELY ALUMINUM SIDING.) BROTHER LANCE, SIS KIM AND ONE OF MANY DOGS.

one hand, and I remember him carrying me on his shoulders. He was constantly hammering, sawing, building, and fixing things. He made our swing and our seesaw and helped Lance build a raft. To me, he was bigger than life.

Daddy's girl from the start, I was the third child of seven. When I arrived—a sporty *and* spunky girl—he was thrilled. In our youth,

I was probably the most athletic of all my brothers and sisters, until the seventh baby, my sister Tracy, was born when I was seven. We are the closest and most alike. The Tweed kids appeared in this order: Lance, Kimberly, Shannon, Sara, Tarry, Jeff, and Tracy. We ranged in coloring from white-blond to carrot-top. Tracy and I were right in the middle: she was a little browner; I was a little redder. Sara and Kim had hair that was nearly white, and Lance and Jeff were blondes. Tarry, the middle boy, had bright red hair.

What were my parents thinking, having seven kids? Happy forever thoughts, I'm sure: they were both hardworking and fun-loving, and life was good for us all.

To me it appeared that my mom and dad were madly in love. He used to chase her around all the time; they were always playing and kissing. Seeing their relationship made a lasting impression on

OUTSIDE THE FRONT DOOR OF THE HOUSE MY DAD AND HIS FRIENDS BUILT, BRICK BY BRICK.

YEA! SOME SNOW OUTSIDE THE MINK SHEDS.

me, setting up an expectation of how it could—or should—be. If they argued or disagreed, I never saw it. My mom was very healthy and energetic. Obviously she had no problems conceiving, and she breezed through her pregnancies and deliveries. She took the attitude: Hey, I've got to do the wash anyway; it's just a bigger load. I'm cooking dinner anyway; it's just more food. I was born in 1957, still a good while before birth control hit the farm. We had cats and dogs everywhere, new puppies and kittens all the time, and kids running around all over the place, somebody always in diapers.

The family finances were constantly fluctuating. My dad's mink ranch was pretty successful until the explosion of fake fur in the sixties. Before and after that, there were times when mink ranching could be very lucrative. Even with seven children, my family was considered reasonably well-off because we lived on a ranch, covering several acres, and were in the process of building a new house. (We lived in my uncle's house on the same property during construction.) In adult terms I have no idea how much money the farm actually made. My dad employed a few ranch hands, and I remember one of them made $35 a week, which sounded like a lot back then.

My dad built our new house, brick by brick, with a little help from our friends. He'd found a pretty spot for us to live, down by a pond. We loved that pond: we played on it, in it, or near it all the time. In the winter beaver would build slides that led down the hill into the water. We'd slip down the beaver slides and hit the ice. When it wasn't thick enough we'd fall through. My mother was constantly running down to fish out one half-frozen kid or another from the water. Also in the winter, Curly, our huge Clydesdale horse who hauled things around the ranch, would pull us kids around on the hood of an old car turned upside down. That was our sleigh—my dad's idea.

In the summertime we picked blueberries and raspberries all over our property and swam in the pond. We never wanted our feet to touch the bottom, because the muck was so deep. There were fish in the muck, and eels, so we'd tread as fast as we could in the water to keep our feet from sinking in. We'd follow the water down to the railroad tracks and find the beavers' dam, and then—typical kids—we'd break it just to see what would happen. We kept an eye on the moose on the other side of the pond that used to emerge to

OUR BACKYARD – THE POND – LANCE WORKING ON BUILDING A WHARF.

drink and eat the bog, sometimes with a family in tow. We'd spot them some early mornings while hooking our fishing lines with fat, juicy earthworms. I always wondered how they could keep their heads up under the weight of those majestic antlers. Early evenings were spent catching frogs and tadpoles.

One hot summer day we noticed that Curly was standing in the water munching and had not moved for quite some time. His legs seemed to be getting shorter and shorter. Finally one of us called,

SHANNON, KIM, LANCE AND MOM IN OUR FRONT YARD.

"Dad, I think Curly's stuck in the bog!" Everyone descended on the pond—my parents, all the kids, and the ranch hands—with the dogs behind us barking frantically. Curly was stuck fast, past his knees, with ducks and geese calmly swimming around him. Even with grown men pulling—and then using a tractor—Curly could not be rescued. After hours of struggling, my dad eventually had to shoo all the kids away and shoot him. It was more humane than leaving Curly to slowly drown, but it was surely one of the saddest things I had ever seen.

Curly's death was a tragic event in my carefree childhood. We were a playful, happy family; someone was always screaming or

11

laughing. Ours was a noisy household with no privacy whatsoever. My older brother, Lance, teased and tickled me until I peed in my pants, and I passed on the favor to my younger brothers, Tarry and Jeff.

My sister Sara was closest in age to me and we played all the traditional games—hide and seek, hopscotch, and skip rope. We went everywhere together. There was a little store called Brown's a couple of miles away from our house where I was occasionally sent to get supplies. On the way to the store I played a game with Sara. She would walk in front of me, and I would put my arms over her shoulders and march behind her, singing a silly little song that went, "Don't be afraid, Lovey, I won't hurt you, Lovey." Periodically I'd whack her on the head. That was the whole game! Eventually we'd make it to the store, where Lance worked pumping gas once he turned 16. The lady who owned the store would let us have one of the empty brown cardboard ice cream tubs that had been scooped out. We'd scrape sweet remnants out of the tub and play the Lovey game, me whacking Sara's head the whole way home. Sara was a sweet little girl, and I don't know why she put up with it. I'm sure I tortured her more than she did me.

I was truly a geeky little girl with pale freckled skin and reddish hair. I was either glow-in-the-dark white or sunburned bright red. Boys never noticed me, and I didn't notice them. You wouldn't have called me "pretty," though of course my parents thought I was. I had a couple of girlfriends who really were pretty, and I envied their flawless, tanned skin and shiny brown hair. In

SNOW DAY WITH FRIENDS OUTSIDE THE MINK SHEDS. IT NEVER GOT
AS COLD AS IT LOOKS.

addition to their looks, my girlfriends had in their favor sandwiches
made with store-bought bread in their lunch boxes every day. I
longed for white bread that looked fancy, with meat from the store
sandwiched between the slices. What I got was homemade bread
spread with margarine, then topped with peanut butter and jam.
Every day the jam dripped through the bread and turned into a
gloppy mess, falling out of its wax paper wrapping. My thermos
leaked and dripped milk all over the contents of my tin lunch box,
turning everything rusty by lunchtime. It was disgusting. I never
ate my lunch—never. I just threw it away and instead ate whatever
candy I could afford to buy or bum from friends. Looking back, I

feel horrible about throwing away the food. Now I crave homemade bread, warm and covered with butter and sugar.

I also sometimes envied the kids we picked up on the bus on our way to school, because they lived close together in groups of houses. I wondered what it would be like to simply run over to the house next door and play. How it would feel to have close neighbors and go in and out of each other's house whenever you wanted. I felt far away from all the action and worried that my girlfriends were growing closer without including me.

My elementary school was in Whitbourne, a community that was far from diverse. All the people I saw growing up were mostly of Irish, English, or Scottish descent. The only difference between neighbors was religion—and believe me, I didn't know the meaning of the word. After school my friends and I used to throw rocks at the Catholic kids, and they at us. We didn't even know why we didn't like them. I don't think I even knew what *Catholic* meant, but someone told me they were "different." How many wars have been fought for that same reason? My parents were not pleased when they heard about my rock throwing, and it stopped shortly afterward. I got spanked once or twice as a kid—I don't remember what for—but this could surely have been one of those instances. I think we were lectured about it in Sunday school, too.

My own family didn't follow any religion in particular. We attended the Salvation Army school, and I went to Sunday school, but not for long. I didn't like going to church because I had to give them my money when the tray came around. We sang songs, and

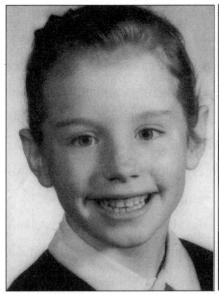 

I STILL HATE MY EARS.   GOT TEETH?

to this day I know every word to "Jesus Loves Me." Apart from the singing, church didn't make much of an impression: I'm not religious at all today. To me as a child, church was somewhere to go that wasn't the ranch, and it was exciting to go anywhere and socialize with the families of kids from school. On Sundays I got to see inside other people's homes, which was always fascinating. Outdoors, while the boys hung around skipping rocks and trying to look cool, the girls got together and played.

Like most little girls, for a short time I really loved Barbie dolls. Since I usually received hula hoops and skipping ropes as gifts, it was a very big treat to get a Barbie doll. I made little clothes for her with my mom's sewing scraps. I loved to dip into the trimmings and button jar my mom kept in the sewing room, next to the kitchen, that was going to be the dining room once the house was finished.

We were supposed to budget our allowance of 25 cents a week so we would have five cents to spend each school day. For a nickel you could buy a pencil or three-for-a-penny candies, gum, and jawbreakers at a little store near the school. I had the odd habit of eating chewed-up gum. If I saw a wad discarded anywhere that looked like it had a little flavor left, I would just pop it in my mouth and chomp away. Right off the ground, I'd pick the dirt out of it and eat it. I cannot imagine why I did this, but I did. I think that's why I have such a strong immune system to this day. What an embarrassing memory. School days of old gum, new pencils, and the Catholics. Rock fights, snowball wars, galoshes over our shoes, soggy sandwiches. Then the weekends came.

I used to sit in trees all the time, particularly on the weekends when I had hours of freedom. My dad made us a swing by hanging an old tire from a tree branch. I liked to escape my brothers and sisters sometimes and have some time alone, so I would climb a tree and just sit there for hours. A few times I climbed too high and my mom had to send my older brother to help me down. (To this day I still enjoy that feeling. I'd like to build a little tree house here at my house in L.A., but I have to say no one is very excited about it but me. "Don't you guys want your very own tree house?" I try to tempt my kids. They can take it or leave it. I would have been so excited to have a tree house as a child, but then again, I don't think my kids are trying to escape anything. Their privacy and their "things" are not forcibly shared or stolen like mine were.)

When I was a kid we all shared everything: clothing, bedrooms—even bathwater. I remember before our house was completed we bathed in shifts in the rinse buckets of the old wringer washer, not changing the water but adding a little more hot after each kid got out and made way for the next. So for me it was nice to find a quiet place to be alone, and when I was by myself, I liked to sing, belting out show tunes and songs I'd heard on the radio in the woods.

If my mom was looking for me, she always found me in a tree or in the woods. As I got older, I used to steal my dad's cigarettes and go out into the woods to smoke—the start of another bad habit. Everyone smoked in the sixties. My dad's brand was Rothman's. They were strong, and smoking them made me so dizzy I felt like

LANCE SARA KIM AND SHANNON. OUR HOMEMADE DRESSES.

I was going to barf. My mother smoked Cameo Menthols, and I liked those better. Sometimes Lance joined me in the woods for a smoke; he picked up the habit, too. Smoking certainly didn't stunt my growth, but to this day, I wish I'd never started.

I developed another bad habit when I graduated to the upper grades and started to attend the school near the bigger town of Dildo. I immediately became totally addicted to Cheetos. I hadn't had much pre-packaged food, and now I was exposed to a cafeteria. I would just toss the food from my lunch box right into the garbage and go straight for the Cheetos, salt-and-vinegar chips, or Sno-balls. It's my theory that if you give your kids a little they're not

NOTE THE NAME OF THE TOWN ON MY DIPLOMA. DILDO?!
COULD THIS BE A SIGN OF THINGS TO COME?

MOM AND DAD'S MOTHER IN THE STORE. IT WAS HERE SHE GATHERED UP GOODIES FOR OUR SPECIAL BIRTHDAY PACKAGES.

going to crave a lot, but if they never have any, they can't wait to get their hands on those little wrappers. I went absolutely wild for all that packaged food, and to this day I have a junk food addiction that will not quit. But now I also appreciate the stews, bread, soups, and other homemade things my mother taught me to make.

My grandfather on my father's side owned a confectionery, a little store in Saskatchewan, and he used to send a box of goodies on each of the kids' birthdays. When mom went into town and came home with that brown box it was so exciting. We knew it was full of candy. We knew some of the contents would be crushed from the journey, but there was always plenty of good stuff left, and there were always fights over who got what. I liked the Sweet

Marie's, O'Henry's, and marshmallow Circus Peanuts. It's one of my fondest memories now—that battered brown box, all the way from Saskatchewan, thousands of miles away from a grandfather and grandmother I didn't know.

As a little girl I wanted to look like the girls in the Sears catalog, even though I actually looked more like Pippi Longstocking. I always had skinned knees, and there was nobody thinner than me. I had freckles all over my skinny little body, and my hair was an unattractive mixture of red, blonde, and brown. At some point I started sleeping in big brush rollers, the kind that hurt your head,

because I thought it was cool, but the curls always turned out very lopsided. School photographs always reflected how little sleep I had gotten the night before and how crooked my freshly cut bangs were. (With seven children, we all took our

ANOTHER NIGHT IN PINCURLS; ANOTHER WACK BANG JOB.

baths at night; so we all slept on our wet hair, which didn't make for pretty pictures, anyway.) My mom eventually showed me how to make pin curls, which were a little easier to sleep on but produced the same hideous result.

That Sears catalog—as a young girl, it really fired my imagination. I started studying the girls in its pages, looking through it and telling myself, "I'm going to be in there someday." I wondered how I could possibly become a model for the Sears catalog; it seemed so glamorous. Those poses—one hand on the hip and one foot pointed out—made the girls look like mannequins. They seemed to me the essence of elegance. I didn't have any conviction that I was pretty enough to model, but I was reasonably sure I could pose like the girls did. I didn't get so far in my daydreams as to think about whether somebody would actually hire me or not. It was all a fantasy.

All us kids pored over the pages of the catalog, making wish lists of the clothes we would buy during our twice-a-year trips to town. My wishes rarely ever came true; there were seven kids, after all. My parents did the best they could. Twice a year my mom packed up three, four, or five of us (whoever was old enough to walk) and drove into town. There were two choices for wardrobe: Woolworth's or Simpson's (as Sears was then known in Canada). These trips were one of the rare times during the year we ate restaurant food; we would have french fries with gravy and sodas at the Woolworth's counter, a much-anticipated treat. (To this day I love fries and gravy with vinegar and ketchup!)

The kids who didn't get hand-me-downs were allowed to pick new clothes, and Mom bought our school uniforms: black lace-up oxfords, white shirts, and, for the girls, little navy pinafore-type dresses. They were dreadful. There were also blazers that we inevitably lost, and, of course, galoshes (we called them rubbers) that went over our shoes to protect them from the muck. The ground was usually very slushy, even though it didn't get brutally cold in our region of Canada. One of the reasons my parents raised mink was that Newfoundland wasn't as cold as the rest of Canada, and the summers weren't as hot. It was a viable place to have rows and rows of sheds that didn't need heat or air-conditioning, but galoshes were a must.

In retrospect I realize that *town* was only 62 miles away. I drive my own kids practically that far every day now taking them to and from school. But in those days it was a big trip. *Town* was where it was at—a very exciting place. Looking back, I also cannot fathom how my mom did it all. I have a nanny for my two kids, and there still aren't enough hours in the day. Seven kids—can you imagine? That's an incredible amount of work just to keep the meals, the clothes, the homework assignments, and the chores straight. The older kids did help, and I was always keeping my eye on one sister or brother so she or he didn't fall in the pond or run down the driveway to the highway. My older sister Kim had the unenviable task of watching out for all of us, which caused rifts between her and me. "You are not the boss of me!" I used to scream at her, and fights would ensue. I even locked her in the basement once when my parents were out, just for spite.

During the time my dad was building our new house, the government sent workers around to start paving the gravel highway that bordered our land. This was a thrilling event. Our ranch lay at the top of a very long driveway, and we would trek down to the highway to take cookies we'd baked to the workmen. How things have changed. I wouldn't let my kids near strangers, but back then, and there, we felt safe. Everyone knew everyone else.

It's a scary world out there now, but when I was a child, out in the country, there was nothing to fear. We thought we didn't have to worry about things like children being kidnapped or sexual predators then. I used to walk to the store two miles away all by myself or with a sibling, before I was seven years old. (Now, in L.A., I live with locks on the doors, dogs, alarms, security systems—everything.) We felt very safe, or maybe I was just sheltered. We didn't have television until I got older—at some point we got a black-and-white TV with two grainy channels. There were no horror stories—nothing except the boogeyman just after the lights went out. Then we loved to scare each other, the girls in one room and the boys in another. We spooked the living daylights out of each other before Mom came in to read to us each night.

We had homemade nightgowns and pin curls. I can still recite the Lord's Prayer.

EARLY MODELING PHOTOS.

CHAPTER TWO

Little Girl Lost

In October 1966 my world came crashing down and my childhood came to an abrupt end. I was nine years old. I'm sure my life would have been completely different if the accident hadn't happened. I would probably never have wandered too far from the ranch. I could easily be sitting in Dildo right now with five kids.

A friend of my dad's bought a brand-new car and drove over to show it off one cold evening. He was anxious to take my dad out for a ride. My dad was really more interested in feeding his horses, but his friend helped him with the chores and persuaded him to come out for a short ride. They wound up at a pub and had a few. While they were relaxing in the pub, snow started to fall, making the roads, which weren't all that great to begin with, much more dangerous.

Who knows what really happened? Maybe they were busy talking and joking and not paying attention; maybe they hit a patch of ice; or maybe they were really too drunk to drive. Whatever the case, they were certainly speeding, going much too fast on winding, narrow country roads. My dad's friend completely missed a treacherous right-hand turn on the familiar road home and slammed the car into a huge rock wall. He was thrown out of the car and died instantly.

My dad was hurled through the windshield and into the branches of a tree, where he hung undiscovered for hours. Nearly every bone in his body was broken. It wasn't until daylight that another car happened along and reported the accident. It initially appeared to be a fatal crash involving only the driver because my dad was nowhere to be seen. The only reason he was found at all was that the rescuers heard a very faint breathing-moaning sound and discovered him tangled up in the tree, barely clinging to life.

Since his injuries were obviously far beyond the scope of the little local hospital where I was born, my dad was taken to the hospital 60 miles away in St. John's. All of the doctors were sure he was going to die, and they concentrated only on keeping him alive minute by minute. He was in a coma, where he remained for a long time, and was certain to have brain damage. He had 19 fractures and stem cell injury; was hooked up to catheters and monitors; laid out on a refrigeration sheet—everything. It was catastrophic.

The days immediately following the accident were a blur. There was a popular song at the time with the line, "Daddy don't you walk so fast." I used to sing that song and cry every night for weeks after my dad's accident. When I went back to school, the other kids and teachers kept coming up to me and offering condolences, and I didn't really understand why. Other people who knew more than I did about the accident were patting me on the shoulder and saying,

MOM AND DAD IN ST. JOHN'S, NEWFOUNDLAND.

"I'm so sorry about your dad," as if he was gone already. He was gone, physically, but not dead. A hole in my heart appeared that I would spend many years trying to fill. It was a terrible, frantic feeling. This was about the time we stopped going to church and reciting the Lord's Prayer each night. I ditched God; where was he when we needed him?

The accident was such a tragedy on every level. Up until the minute it happened, my mom and dad were still crazy about each other; they were always having fun together, whooping it up. Whenever one of us burst into their room in the mornings they'd have to scramble to get decent. He was always smacking her behind when she walked past and grabbing her and kissing her. That was my frame of reference for how a marriage should be. It was what I wanted in a partner. I wanted someone to adore me, and I looked for it forever. But for my mom that ideal husband was no more.

The entire structure of our lives was gone. My parents had been an excellent team in every way. My mom's job had been to raise the kids, keep house, and do the bookkeeping for the ranch. My dad's job had been to provide for us and do the manual labor. After the accident, my mom had to take on the physical outdoor work as well as run the whole operation.

Daddy was allowed to come home after several months in the hospital. He emerged from his coma a very angry man. He was not the father I remembered; he had become an entirely different person. He had good reason to be angry: to him, it seemed that he woke up one day and his seven children and ranch were all gone, never to return. He now behaved like a very angry, confused child. He and my mother fought. There was no kissing anymore. No laughter, no hugs, very little hope. If I had been in my mother's place, I would have killed myself. That was a lot for one woman to bear.

I'm sure my parents had many anguished discussions, with my mom saying things like "I can't do this alone—the ranch, the business, seven kids—what am I supposed to do now? I have to sell; I have to leave." My father was dead set against it. It was his ranch, his whole life, and his livelihood that he had worked so hard to build from nothing. I can imagine that fight as an adult, but they were good about sheltering us from all the tension. As a nine-year-old all I knew was we lived on a ranch, Daddy had an accident, and now we were going to have to leave.

My dad was only home for two weeks in a wheelchair before he had to return to the hospital for an extended period of time. It was now clear he would survive, and the doctors had to work on those bones not properly set when they were so sure he would die. He had a very long rehabilitation ahead, including months of strenuous physical therapy.

The brain injuries my father sustained were similar to those of a stroke victim—he had to learn how to walk and talk and drive again. It was fascinating, in a scary way, to see his inability to hide any of his

DONALD KEITH TWEED. PORTRAIT OF A BROKEN MAN: DAD AFTER THE ACCIDENT ON A VISITATION DAY.

feelings after the accident. I believe that our family life might have been salvaged if he had been able to keep his emotions in check, but my dad could not stop whatever he was thinking or feeling from coming out of his mouth. He no longer had a filter. His personality had irrevocably changed. It was heartbreaking to see my strong, vibrant father turned into this angry, crippled mess in a wheelchair.

All these abrupt changes were devastating to me and, I'm sure, to my siblings. I was the only family member my dad would tolerate coming near him when he came home for his visit in between operations and rehabilitation, and he needed a lot of help. He wouldn't allow anyone else to take him to the bathroom or help him walk. He was so heavy. I remember him leaning on Mom and me—he clung to me, and I couldn't understand why. I was just an ordinary little girl, one whose daddy was now gone—there physically, but his essence was gone forever. However, there was something about me he liked and things about some of the other kids he now hated and verbalized. The outbursts were due to the brain trauma, but it was incredibly hurtful, especially to my brothers, to have their father not like them anymore and say cruel things to them. My brothers were careful to never get too close. The whole thing was bizarre and emotionally upsetting. I knew he didn't really mean his harsh words, but it made me cry all the time—for them, for him, and for all of us.

For a while after my dad's accident, my mother, friends, and the ranch hands managed, but it was the sixties in rural Canada, and the banks took a dim view of a woman's ability to run a ranch and refused to lend her enough money to keep things going. Nor did my mother's parents offer any real financial help. They were prosperous motel owners, but I believe there was a bit of bad blood in the family history—some bitterness left over from years before, when my mom had left Saskatchewan as a young woman and gone off with my father to some godforsaken place to raise mink. There was nothing left to do but sell the ranch.

During all this, of course, I still had to go to school every day and carry on, as much as possible, with my regular routine. I developed a very intense crush on my fifth-grade female teacher. I can't remember her name, but I can still see her so clearly: she was young, with dark hair and brown eyes, and she had a petite little frame. My teacher treated all of her students with loving attention and was so kind that I always wanted to be near her.

As fifth grade turned to sixth, my affections

THIS SCHOOL PHOTO HIGHLIGHTED THE GAP BETWEEN MY TWO FRONT TEETH NICELY, DON'T YOU THINK? ONCE AGAIN, MOM MADE MY OUTFIT.

soon turned to one of my friend's older brothers. Billy played the bass for a local band and was just dreamy-looking. He had dark hair, brown eyes, and some color in his skin. He was dark Irish. His skin was beautiful—unlike mine. (My whole life I've had skin problems. I've always been the girl with the pimple. I had very oily skin, and my mom promised I would stop breaking out when I got older. Well, I'm almost 50 now, and I'm ready for it to stop, but it hasn't.) Billy was different from me, and I liked different in a boy. I like opposite.

I am sure my father's accident played a large part in why I was so desperate for this boy to like me—though maybe it was just hormones, or both. I dreamed of him taking me to the local drive-in or to the soda shop—anything, but whenever I was around, Billy would walk right by me like I wasn't there.

The first time I was allowed to go to a local teen dance I walked with my older brother and sister the two miles to town. The dance was being held in the Whitbourne billiard hall. I must have been the biggest geek. I remember standing there and just staring at Billy during the dance while he played bass with his band. I'm sure he saw me fixated on him and just thought, *Oh God, get her out of here*. He was much older, 16. Halfway through the dance I had to go home; I had an 11-year-old's curfew. Just to get rid of me, I'm sure, Billy took me outside for a walk. He kissed me on the forehead and said good-bye. It was a brush-off, but I was on cloud nine. He had kissed me! On the forehead! I was so excited, I thought about that kiss every day for an entire year. But I never saw him again after the dance, because soon after that we moved away.

My parents' marriage was effectively over. With no help forthcoming from anyone, my mom had no choice but to sell the ranch. It was decided that we were moving to Saskatchewan without my father, where my mother's sister had a home and family. The three oldest children would be sent ahead to live with my aunt and uncle for a few months, while my mom shut down the whole operation and joined us later with the four younger kids.

The first to leave were Kim, Lance, and me. I left behind my two best friends, Diane and Betty Russell, cousins who had been my girlfriends all through elementary school. Diane and I were closer friends, and she, too, was my opposite—dark hair, brown eyes, olive skin—the friend I had always thought was so beautiful. Once we moved from the ranch, everything was in such turmoil. It never even occurred to me to write letters to my friends or try to stay in touch. It was a clean break; once we got to Saskatchewan we all started over. New school; new home. Not ours, but new.

The big song on the radio at that time started with the lines "Which way you goin' Billy? Can I go too?" The song echoed in my mind and made me cry as I boarded a plane for the very first time. From Newfoundland to Saskatchewan was a major move. I cried for most of the flight but stopped when I was served soft rolls and butter for the first time ever. I could not get enough of airplane food (which I like to this day). I said, "My gosh, this is so delicious; what is it?" My aunt was surprised. "Honey," she answered gently, "it's butter?" Well, we'd never had butter at home. I'm sure at one church gathering or another I must have tasted butter, but my mother used to buy margarine or lard in bulk. I stuffed my face as tears rolled down my cheeks, the beginning of consoling myself with food.

In the weeks to come I would miss my dog, Lassie, and my cat, Harold. I would miss my mom's homemade bread, the fresh fried-and-sugarcoated doughnuts she made. I'd miss watching her knead the dough and giving us some to play with. I'd miss homemade Play-Doh and homemade clothes. I'd miss the woods and fishing and the smells of home; the thump of the old wringer washer and the hum of the sewing machine. Most of all I'd miss the sight of my dad coming home after a hard day at work, and being allowed to put five teaspoons of sugar in his coffee and tasting it for him.

My old life...and my childhood... were gone.

CHAPTER THREE

Rebel Just Because

My mom somehow managed to keep us off welfare—barely. I've really got to hand it to her; she could easily have copped out and said, "I can't take possibly care of these seven kids all alone." But she never said "Poor me"—at least not out loud. It was a horrible time for her. The love of her life was gone. My angry, embittered dad was still in the hospital for rehabilitation, and she was trying to pay off what bills she could. Her three oldest kids were gone, and she still was taking care of the four little ones while closing down the ranch. I don't know how she managed. I would have been hanging from the rafters.

It was a chaotic time for everyone. While my mom was getting her affairs in order, I was trying to adjust to life in a new place with my uncle's family. I went from swooning over Billy kissing me on the forehead to developing a fierce crush on my cousin Randy. How backward of me! I was only 12 and I didn't do anything about it, but oh, I loved him. He, like Billy, was tall, dark, and handsome. I

MY COUSIN RANDY – I HAD A CRUSH ON HIM!

became fixated on him while Lance, Kim, and I were living in their house. My aunt and uncle did their best to be surrogate parents, but I was a confused, hormonal preteen and didn't notice or appreciate their efforts. I started at a new school and began making new friends. I got my first job, grooming horses with my cousin Brenda, who I'm sure wasn't thrilled that I was tagging along. She was paid with riding, and I was paid with a little bit of heaven: Rice Krispies with fresh heavy cream and brown sugar. Wow, that was good!

Eventually the whole family—minus my dad—got back together. It was an entirely new way of life for all of us. We were in a city now, which was quite a change from a mink ranch. Our new home was one of a group of three-story row houses with fixed rents for low-income families.

I attended Carolyn Robbins, a very forward-thinking school. They had classes in the round, with all the students sitting on the floor in a circle with the teacher, who was also part of the circle. The classes were all held in the one room. It was very interesting. As a student, I was like most kids—good in the subjects I enjoyed. I liked creative writing and math a lot, and every school I attended had some kind of choir I joined.

We walked the four blocks to and from school each day, back to the low-rent part of town where we lived. My mom worked days and went back to school at night. She enrolled in a lab technology course

MOM AND HER BROOD AT 71 WESTVIEW PLACE; SASKATOON, SASK., CANADA. LANCE, MOM, KIM, SHANNON, SARA, TARRY, JEFF AND TRACY. DID MY MOM KNOW I WAS OUT IN A VOLKSWAGEN WITH MURRAY?

in 1970; in fact, she and my sister Tracy started school on the same day. Mom had trained as a nurse before getting married, but now, without much help from her parents, she had to manage to support all of us. (Mom would eventually specialize in hematology and in 1981 became the director of administration for the laboratories at Royal University Hospital and the Department of Pathology for the College of Medicine at University of Saskatchewan.)

My mother was doing remarkably well managing her new circumstances, but work and school didn't leave her much time for her kids. Mom did the best she could; I would never find fault with her in any way for anything she did, but I wish she could have encouraged us to keep in touch with Dad. I think it would have helped me and the other kids. In hindsight I assume that it was too emotionally painful for Mom and Dad to have any contact. I was now a girl with a big piece of my heart missing. Ever since the accident I've been standing on chairs trying to get men to love me. I did everything I could to get their attention. My dad had really loved me, and I missed basking in his adoration. I was going to find that feeling again, any way I could.

A photographer snapped a picture of me one day, catching me right at the beginning of my rebellious period. There was a sign on the street that said, "No Standing No Stopping," and the local newspaper published a photo of me standing under the sign hitchhiking. Meanwhile, my mom told me not to ever do anything like that. I wasn't supposed to be hitching rides or hanging at the mall, but now I was, in a word, busted!

I started shoplifting at the local drugstore and at stores in the mall after school. I got caught at the mall, and my mom had to come bail me out of jail. The mall security actually took me to the police station to throw some fear into me. The idea was to scare kids so badly they'd never do it again. In my case, it worked. My friends and I kept hanging out at the drugstore and the mall, but I would never steal again.

I started acting out in other ways, too. No more silent crushes, like on Billy and Randy. I acquired my first real boyfriend—in retrospect, he was probably a pervert. He was an older boy from another school—high school—and he was cruising the middle

MY FRIEND LAURIE LYMAN, DUNCAN MACKENZIE (ANOTHER EX-BOYFRIEND!)
MY SISTER KIM AND ME AND CHRISTMAS. STYLIN', WASN'T I?

school grounds for chicks! Murray was 17 years old, and I was 13. He had a load of curly, sandy blond hair and drove a little Volkswagen as blue as his eyes. I thought he was so handsome and was flattered when he paid attention to me. So, what did I do when he started talking to me? I jumped right in the car! All my friends egged me on: "Oooooh! An older boyfriend! Is Murray picking you up tonight?" My mom did not have a clue about what was going on between me and Murray or she would have put a quick stop to it, but she was distracted by the six other kids, a full-time job, and lab classes all vying for her attention.

Murray introduced me to oral sex, which I must say was great. Being on the receiving end, that is—I was far too young and inexperienced to reciprocate. Come to think of it, I believe he was perfecting his technique, practicing on me. In a Volkswagen Bug, mind you. I was so young; I look back on this and know it was wrong. I would be horrified if my daughter ever did anything like that, not to mention I would have to kill the guy too! But no one was watching, no one was keeping an eye on me. There was a woman, Mrs. Rennieberg, who came over to make meals for us while my mom was at work. I had never liked liver and onions until Mrs. Rennieberg made it for me. (I ate a lot of Kraft Macaroni & Cheese and liver in those days.) She fed us, but that was as far as it went. I was unsupervised! All I could think about was Murray. Did he really like me? Was I in love?

I can't remember if I ever introduced Murray to my mother.

I used to stay out late with him and tell her I was at my friend Laurie's house. Laurie lived in the same housing project we did, and it would have been pretty easy for my mom to walk over and check, but she never did. Poor mom—she had all those kids, all those worries, and I was off with some boy in a Volkswagen.

At his age—17—it really wasn't right for Murray to do what he was doing with me, but it could have been much worse. He could have used and abused me and been violent and ugly, but he wasn't like that at all. He was very considerate. We never really went anywhere. He'd pick me up and we'd kiss until our lips were raw. Just sit and neck for hours and hours. He definitely paid me a lot of attention, at a time when I was yearning for it. I don't know whatever happened to Murray. We lost touch after I left eighth grade and started high school. Maybe I got too old for him!

In ninth grade, I developed a big crush on a football player. His name was Brian, and he took me to a party. It was the first time my mother got involved on a personal level in my romantic life. She made me a kelly-green dress to wear. I only had that one date with Brian. I have blocked out

CHRIS DEAN, WE DATED. HE WROTE SWEET LOVE LETTERS FROM ENGLAND BUT NEVER CAME BACK!

EYE MAKEUP AND 70'S FASHION AT THE MALL.

the details of what happened, but I clearly recall walking home alone from the party. I knew that night he would never ask me out again, and he didn't. I had no clue how to be cool, how to behave.

That same year, I fell for another guy with a Volkswagen Bug, but I never could get him to respond to me. His name was Eddie, and he was a hippie. I used to hang out with all his hippie friends at the mall, wanting so much to get close to Eddie, but he was stoned all the time. He smoked pot constantly, and I never enjoyed smoking pot. It just made me hungry, and detached from reality. I wanted to be in my right mind. But still I hung out with all these potheads instead of going to school, waiting in vain for Eddie to pay me some attention, skipping my classes and smoking cigarettes.

My teenage years were forming a very distinct pattern. My life was all about going from boyfriend to boyfriend, because my whole life has been about finding the guy. Finding my dad, the love that I lost. Don't get me wrong, I had some lasting good girlfriends, too, but they were just as boy crazy as I was. Besides clothes and makeup—neither of which I had much of—boys were all we talked about.

My friends from the housing district were Laurie (my sleepover partner in crime), Wanda, Cheryl and their sister Helen. The oldest was Helen, but the genetics in that family were phenomenal. What great bodies they had! I was jealous of their well-developed busts and butts—mine wouldn't ripen until much later. Apparently, however, I was grown-up enough for Helen's boyfriend, Andy, the son of a doctor. I went to a party at his house and lost my virginity to him in a five-minute fit of drunken passion. I never saw him again and always regretted giving that special gift to someone I didn't love and who didn't love me.

While I was still in ninth grade, I met my next serious boyfriend through my older brother. Lance had set up his own living area in the basement of our town house. He had a mattress on the floor next to his stereo and was always down there with his friends listening to music. His best friend was a Ukrainian guy named John, who was—surprise!—very into oral sex. John lived with his mother, naturally enough, because he was still in high school. I used to sleep over at his house all the time—in his room, in his bed, any night of the week and walk home in the wee hours of the morning before my mother got up. I remember meeting his mother. She just looked at me and asked Johnny something in Ukrainian. He answered, and she shook her head...and fired off a lot more rapid Ukrainian that I could not understand. I'm sure she was asking John, "What does her mother say?" or "Why is she here; you can't sleep with a girl with no birth control! You two are going to wind up with a baby!"

Johnny had a powder blue '67 Mustang he used to let me drive. He was a good, straight kid who went off to class every day while I cruised around in his car. I would drive around all day in his Mustang, hang out with the hippies at the mall, and pick John up after school. I don't know what either one of us was thinking... I didn't have a license!

My relationships with boys at the time did have some positive effect on my self-esteem. John was a budding artist and drew a portrait of me. After he presented it and I had the chance to study it carefully, I thought for the first time that I wasn't bad-looking. If John thought I was pretty, maybe I really was pretty. Murray had thought I was pretty, too. I started thinking, *Hmmmm. Okay, maybe...* and started plucking my eyebrows and wearing a little makeup.

☙ ☙ ☙

When I was 15, Johnny and I broke up, and I headed into tenth grade by the skin of my teeth. I was barely passing. One of my girlfriends, Lynn, liked my brother Lance, and we got pretty close. We used to sit in the washroom at school smoking cigarettes. The teachers had to know that we were sitting in the bathroom smoking. I'm sure it smelled up the whole school. But everybody smoked then; it was no big deal. There I was in a washroom in a school in Saskatchewan, speculating with my friend on the chances

ME AND TRACY SITTING ON THE NEIGHBORS' STOOP. WE STILL CAN'T OPEN OUR PALE BLUE EYES IN THE SUN.

of us making a go of it as hookers, rationalizing that because if we liked having sex for free, why not get paid for it? (Lynn ended up staying in school, going to university, and doing very well, though sadly, she was diagnosed early in life with multiple sclerosis.)

I never took up prostitution, thank God, but my mind was obviously elsewhere, and eventually I dropped out of high school altogether. My memory of exactly when I left school is vague, but my mother reminds me that I was only one semester short of graduation. There was no conscious decision to quit, but clearly my heart wasn't in it, and I had missed so much school, so many days in a row, that I eventually just never went back. I got a job as a hostess in a nightclub. It was illegal because I was underage, but I lied and said I was 18, and no one had any reason to doubt me. The owner of the club was another pervert—and I mean that in the nicest way possible—tall, dark, handsome, and worldly.

Certainly there was a part of me that was always attracted to this type of man, but this particular club owner was much older, probably 35 or so, which was ancient to me since I was still 16. We had brief intimate moments until I turned 17 and met a devastatingly good-looking guy with a mustache from Holland at the club. We started seeing each other regularly. He was a window dresser at one of the department stores in town, and he wanted to "fix" me. He drank heavily and was highly critical of me, but I loved him, and we did things together that didn't involve sex: cooking, decorating, fishing, and traveling. He even bought me my first real "ensemble," a cream-colored knit three-piece skirt suit. He was very fashion savvy. Bob E. even took me to visit my father for the first time—we took a road trip in a green Vega. It took having that support—and cash—behind me to get me there. The three of us shared a joyful long weekend until Bob had to get back to work. I was grateful to him for opening up the lines of communication between me and my father again.

Bob E. and I stayed together for a while, and I worked in all kinds of places: bars, a tie store, the shoe department of an Army/Navy store, a hotel, a ski resort, even pumping gas on the graveyard shift at a Mohawk gas station. I think at that time my boyfriend was still completely unaware of his true sexual orientation, or at the very

MY FIRST GABARDINE SUIT

Bob and I, very fashionable at the time. He bought me my first gabardine suit.

Bob and me roasting a pig and fishing in northern Ontario.

THE OH-SO-HANDSOME AND TROUBLED BOB EGELIE WITH ME IN HOLLAND AT THE WEDDING OF HIS SISTER. DON'T REMEMBER WHO THE BABY BELONGS TO.

least couldn't bring himself to admit his true preferences. He had a mustache, but I was the beard. When his employer transferred him to Ottawa, the capital of Canada, he took me with him—after a trip to Holland to attend his sister's wedding. I was getting somewhere, little by little. Somewhere else—I always wanted to be somewhere else.

Immediately after arriving in Ottawa I got pregnant, though certainly not on purpose. Bob E. was clearly not pleased; nor was I. The details of making all the arrangements are a bit fuzzy, but through a friend of mine and a friend of his I was somehow shuffled one night onto a bus to New York for an abortion. I had to scrape all my money together, get on some bus, and go to New York alone. I mean, *New York? Me? The little farm girl from Canada?* It was crowded with young women going down to the big city to get abortions. On the ride back I was bleeding heavily, but I changed clothes in our apartment and went right to work at my job as a cocktail waitress at an upscale hotel bar the next day.

It wasn't a bad job. People in that government town usually got off work around three-thirty in the afternoon, and they'd hit the bars and start drinking. At some point the other waitresses and I would stop taking orders, grab beer from the bar, and go out and sell them, because it was too crowded to take individual orders. I developed really strong right-arm muscles because my tray was always so heavily loaded down with beer. After a while my tray would be weighted down with money, stacks and stacks of bills with beer spills all over it—and I was still too young to even be served in a bar, much less work in one. The money was great—the money we made and the money we stole, after we lost count and our good judgment.

It was just another night at work when I returned from New York. I was feeling okay. I put on my little outfit, cut up to here and down to there, with legs forever. But I was also wearing tons of pads because I was bleeding so heavily, and I'm sure it looked like I was wearing a diaper. All of a sudden, in the middle of my shift, I felt kind of woozy.

A regular customer of mine, a really handsome Lebanese man named Henry, someone I'd always liked, came up to me. He said, "Hey, are you okay? You don't look so good. Let me take you home." Well, his intentions were kind of good: he took me to

ROBERTO HERRERA IN OTTAWA – WHAT A GREAT KISSER!

his home. We talked for awhile about the problems I was having with my boyfriend and he told me how much he'd always liked me. Then I had sex with him. I was confused and needy, and on some level I appreciated him "saving" me. He didn't know what I'd done that week, but he knew something wasn't quite right. I started bleeding heavily later that evening. Henry called a doctor for me and took me to the hospital, where I was given blood and fluids. I recuperated and kept the new doctor as my gynecologist.

On the pill now; no more mistakes, except I was still incredibly naïve. My new doctor, the one I'd turned to for help, came on to me and we started an affair. That was wrong on so many levels. I mean, honestly, what were all these guys thinking? An 18-year-old girl, and all they could think about was getting off—and one of them a doctor! I look back at those days and wonder at what point does abuse start? When are you being used as opposed to using someone? It's always been a very blurry line for me. Am I driving the car, or is the car driving me?

THIS PHOTO WAS TAKEN FOR *PLAYBOY* BY RICHARD FEGELY. I MISS HIM –
HE TOOK MOST OF MY PHOTOS FOR *PLAYBOY* AND WAS THE PHOTOGRAPHER
SCOUTING IN TORONTO WHEN I ASKED MY AGENT TO TEST.

Playmate for Life

I was angry that, even though this was the seventies, the man who had gotten me pregnant wasn't even sympathetic. My Dutch boy was soon gone; he ran off with some other window dresser. His new boyfriend was not an attractive man. I was so damn insulted. Not only did he leave me for a guy...but a really ugly guy! I used to see them around town once in awhile after we split, and it always just burned me up. But I felt stronger, and it was time for me to find my own place and make a go of it on my own.

Ottawa was a much more diverse community than the smaller towns I was used to. It had a big Lebanese population, and with my new strength intact, I started working for a Lebanese family at a little coffee shop during the daytime. I was the best waitress you've ever seen. Without pilfering, I made plenty of money by just raking in tips. I wasn't afraid to work hard, and I was fast. The owner's son and cook, Eddie, who managed the coffee shop, fell madly in love with me. He really liked my work ethic, plus I was a pretty girl,

EDDIE, MY LOVE, BEFORE HE CHEATED WITH THE WAITRESSES AT SHANNON'S BAR.

making money for his shop like you wouldn't believe. He couldn't believe his good luck. He was crazy about me. We laughed about everything and were together all the time. He cooked; I served. We played house.

As I was going about my work there I met another Lebanese man who owned a modeling agency. He asked me if I would like to enter the Miss Ottawa pageant, which was preliminary to the Miss Canada competition. I said, "Well, I don't know...," and he said, "Come on, let's do it!" Soon enough, he talked me into it.

I was barely 18 years old. I had quit school and left home with a gay guy. Obviously, to qualify for the Miss Ottawa pageant you were supposed to be a graduate of some high school, somewhere! So I lied again, and no one checked. There were no computers back then; it was easy to get away with. And what was my talent? Well, I decided I would sing. I'd never had any training or a particularly musical background, apart from choir in school and listening to my mother's beautiful voice. I just got up there on stage and sang. The judges liked me, and I won the Miss Ottawa crown. I was headed for Miss Canada.

THE MISS CANADA PAGEANT 1978. THEY CUT AND PERMED MY HAIR DAYS BEFORE THE BROADCAST. I WAS SICK ABOUT IT!

FISHING IN KEY WEST. I WENT THERE WITH MY CUBAN BOYFRIEND
ROBERTO. OUR GUIDE HOLDS UP THE BARRACUDA I CAUGHT.

By winning the pageant, I gained a certain amount of celebrity
in Ottawa and started modeling, locally at first. So my boss/
boyfriend Eddie opened a bar in my name. I was now part-owner
of a bar called Shannon's. I started bartending and learned to make
every drink imaginable. I don't even know what kinds of drinks are
popular now, but back then I was good. I would pour and shake and
mix it up, the girls would pick up the drinks and sell them, and we'd
do great business.

Eddie and I lasted a good while. He was quite a character. He
used to buy hot jewelry for me all the time from shady characters
in trench coats who hung out at the club. To look at him, you
wouldn't think he could get all the girls, but he had a way about

him. I was great friends with one of the waitresses, Dagmar from Germany, until I found out she was fooling around with him. It was time to get out of there. I had started to get a few additional little modeling jobs here and there in Montreal and Toronto, and I was thinking of moving to a bigger city permanently. For the moment, I stayed in my little attic apartment, where I used to hit my head on the slanted stone ceiling.

I was seeing a Cuban guy off and on who had a graphic design business. Roberto taught me to make dulce de leche. I haven't made it since, but I've thought of him and wondered if he ever made up with his wife. He was separated and tortured, and I was comforting.

My move finally came when I met a new guy who used to come into Shannon's all the time. He was a Canadian Football League linebacker from the South—Alabama, maybe? Ronnie Fox was his name, and he was a humongous black guy with a great body and a fab sense of humor. He was traded to Toronto, and when he left, I went with him. (Another man; another bigger city. Why was it I could never go anywhere by myself?)

It was an exciting move for me. Toronto was—and is—Canada's most cosmopolitan city. Sensing something big was going to happen for me there, I called my father and told him about the move. He was happy for me and glad that I was a little closer to him geographically. I mentioned that it would be easier for me to visit him, and told Dad about my modeling gigs and about Ron. He told me that he'd found love again, too. His caregiver was now his

MY FOOTBALL PLAYER, RONNIE FOX.

girlfriend, and he seemed in good spirits; I was happy to know he wasn't alone.

Through my Ottawa agency I landed a modeling agent in Toronto. I had appeared in some Canadian publications and some big department store ads (The Hudson Bay Co., Fairweather, and—at last—Sears), but I was still waitressing to supplement my income. It was tough to get by in Toronto on modeling alone. By this time I had been slinging beer for six years, and I was sick of it. Toronto was not a hot spot where I could make a lot of money as a model. I was living with Ron and working, but I craved money, advancement, and opportunity. Ron lent me his van while he was at football practice to go on auditions, and I soon got used to

EARLY MODELING.

EARLY MODELING HEAD SHOT.

rejection—a talent that would come in handy in Hollywood.

When I heard a *Playboy* photographer was coming to town I asked to be tested. Another girl at my agency was trying out, and I wanted to as well. The other girl wound up appearing on the cover. I also knew of another girl from Montreal whose photograph had been in *Playboy*. She had a very exotic look and was able to continue a fairly successful modeling career afterward. I realize now that I didn't meet the criterion for a high-fashion print model: I was okay-looking but didn't really jump off the page. I didn't have that *oomph*, but I modeled a little, waitressed a lot, and got by.

I tested three separate times for *Playboy*. At this point in time—the early eighties—Hugh Hefner was still very hands-on with the magazine, and he reviewed every set of test shots himself. He turned down my pictures more than once. Two thumbs down, twice in a row. It was always something: too this, too that... One criticism was that I was too skinny. Skinny was my natural state; I never had to diet. My whole family was tall and thin.

By the third time around I had gotten to know the *Playboy* photographer, Richard Fegely. He said, "Shannon, we're getting you in. I don't care how long it takes." We were determined that I would get into *Playboy*. I started eating more, got a little more voluptuous-looking, and on the third time I hit the jackpot; I was chosen for *Playboy*. I was Miss November 1981. And you know what? It's the ugliest layout I have ever seen. The girls in *Playboy* always looked so sexy, and I looked young and innocent, like the girl next door. The glamour part of me certainly didn't kick in until

MODELING IN MONTREAL.

long after I moved to L.A. and learned a few tricks of the trade.

Appearing in *Playboy* was such a scandalous thing back then, especially coming from where I came from. My dad, bless his heart, was all for it. He was totally supportive. When I told him about it he said, "Hell yeah, go for it. What are you waiting for, a car to hit you?" That certainly put it all into perspective for me. Anyone could have an accident like his any day of their life. Life's all about taking chances. Living your best life. Doing what makes you happy. I wasn't going to worry about what other people thought. No one was going to stop me from having adventures.

Dad had been recuperating well, and it was ironic that just as he was about to have his driver's license reinstated, he died of angina before the November issue actually came out. But he knew all about it, and I'm sorry that he never saw my layout. Not that I wanted my dad to view naked photos of me, but I would have loved for him to see *Playboy* and know that I had done it, that I was going for it, whatever "it" was!

After my initial visit to the Mansion for the Midsummer Night's Dream party where I met Hef for the first time, I started coming to L.A. on frequent trips from Toronto and getting friendlier with everyone. The second or third time I was there, Hef called me in to the library and sat me down. He said, "Sondra and I were wondering...," and I thought, "Oh, my God. Here it comes. What is my answer going to be?" Because I knew what the question was. I was petrified and excited at the same time. The Playboy Mansion was a completely different environment from anywhere else. It was so secluded and private, a whole other world. You could basically start over once you got inside the gate, which was very attractive to me at this point in my life. In those days there were no paparazzi, no public photos; the gossip never traveled beyond the immediate little world of Playboy Mansion West—probably because whoever you were with didn't want anyone to know, either.

The question was on the table: "Would you consider spending some time with us?" And I answered yes. Why not?—I had an open mind; I had nothing to lose. Christ, I could say no, and do what? Go back home to Canada? Or say yes, and see what developed. So I said sure. I stayed for a little while, spent some time with both of

FINALLY THAT SEARS AD!

FINALLY THAT
SEARS AD!

them, then headed home. I still had Ronnie, my boyfriend back in Toronto—though clearly I wasn't too serious about him. He was getting very nervous, because the writing was on the wall.

One day soon after I had returned to Canada, I got a message on my answering machine that said, "Hi darling, this is Hef. I really miss you and was wondering if you'd come down here and live with me." He had made the decision to let Sondra go. He wanted me to be his main girlfriend. Though I didn't have any idea what that would entail, I was still thrilled. I flew down in a heartbeat. I left my car behind—the first car I had ever owned, a little Mazda, bought with my Playmate money. Later, when Hef had gotten to know me better, he thought that I would be a good candidate for Playmate of the Year. I couldn't believe it when he broke the news. I knew that

Red Fox

Modeling furs, of course, in Canada.

the Playmate of the Year was given one hundred thousand dollars and a new Porsche. I was over the moon. Plus, I got the guy! I was hardly off that mink ranch, and here I had the car, the money, the guy, and a new life in L.A.!

Unfortunately, neither Sondra nor Ronnie could see the beauty of this new situation. Ron was not happy, and we parted. Even though he wound up playing football somewhere in the United States, we eventually lost touch. I'm sure Sondra felt betrayed, like I had plotted the whole thing out. But really, I had fallen in love, and so had Hef. I'm sure she must have known that nothing permanent would come from a love affair with the most confirmed bachelor in the world. I certainly didn't think that way, but I wasn't about to miss this ride, wherever it was going.

PHOTOGRAPHIE: GERALDO PACE

CHAPTER FIVE

One and a Hef

It was a very heady, exciting ride. It was wild, fast and loose. No one had heard of AIDS, word on the street was that cocaine wasn't addictive, and smoking and drinking were the norm. There was a carefree feeling of "Why not?" It was a different era. Nowadays you really have to think about who you're with, because you're taking your life in your hands having sex with somebody new; you're sleeping with every person they ever slept with. Those thoughts just weren't present at that time. "Hell yeah, I'm there!" was my attitude.

Usually I thought that whatever people were getting from me, I was getting something in return; it's a mutual give-and-get situation. It was that way with Hef, too. I certainly never thought he was going to marry me. That wasn't the deal, though for a time in the back of this girl's mind was the thought that it wouldn't be out of the question for me. But truly, it wasn't that kind of relationship. It was sexual attention and excitement and good times, though I can honestly say I loved him. Not in the same way I love Gene, not the way you love the father of your children, when you know that you

PUBLICITY PHOTO FOR MY PLAYMATE OF THE YEAR 1981.

MOM, ME AND TRACY AT THE PLAYMATE OF THE YEAR LUNCHEON.

want to be with him forever. Even living at the Playboy Mansion I could see the day when sitting around, partying, drinking, and doing whatever nonsense we felt like doing was not going to be all that I needed. The relationship didn't have that permanent feeling. It was intense in a different way. It was all so shiny and new and thrilling. I didn't know what I wanted to do or be, but I thought this was certainly a good start. A lot of girls who pose for *Playboy* think that's the be all to end all—the pinnacle, the big prize. Not me. It was just the beginning of a whole new life for me.

I now had what was practically my very own father figure as a devoted love interest and all new friends. No one in L.A. knew (or cared) anything about what I had done before. They had no preconceived notions about what I was like or what I should do. I was completely new in a new country, starting over. I skipped most of my publicity tour for Playmate of the Year because Hef didn't want me out of his sight. To this day I think I won Playmate of the Year because back in those days Hef made the final decision. I'm glad it worked that way, because my pictures were much different than the other eleven girls. I wasn't voluptuous or sexy-looking. I wasn't a raunchy, sexy babe from California, all tanned and toned, ripping off my bikini in the pictures. I mean, we grew our pubic hair in so people wouldn't see too much! That was the Canadian way—cover up!

My attitudes were all turning and changing. Now I was running around half-naked all the time and feeling great about it. It was very liberating. There is a certain conservative part of Canada that was so British, and to an extent still is, and that mindset was (and is) still with me. You don't do that. *What would the neighbors think? Nice girls don't...*

I was learning that nice girls do. And you know what? Sometimes nice girls do it better. All these girls were nice—all these people are nice, and we do. And we're gonna, and I'm gonna! And we did. We partied all night and slept all day, and just generally did whatever we felt like at the time with whomever we felt like. "Love the one you're with!"

However, my warning lights came on when I started to drink quite a bit. It was no surprise, given the history of alcohol abuse in

AD FOR BEAUTY PRODUCTS.

my family, that I liked to drink. Shots, beers, B-52s, and things we mixed up and invented—I had a very high tolerance for alcohol, something I hadn't previously been aware of, because I hadn't ever imbibed much before. Well, my Dutch boyfriend and I had done some drinking, but before I hit California there hadn't been much major partying in my life. This was a whole new level of hedonism.

I also started experimenting with cocaine, which wasn't anything Hef encouraged or endorsed. He wasn't very happy about it, but I was having a fine time. My friends and I all did cocaine to stay up and drank to fall asleep. It was a vicious circle, but we were young and stupid and didn't feel any worse for the wear. When you're 24 years old and get loaded, it's not like you need to take time to recover. And you look fine, too. Those were wild, wild times; I saw the most incredible things going on. They probably were not that wild compared to today's L.A. standards, but imagine how I felt, seeing a guy with two girls in the swimming pool, while I sat up on the roof spying, cracking up... *Wow, look at that; look at that!* Usually it was someone famous, and by that I mean extremely famous, the kind of person easily recognizable by most American people.

It was quite interesting to see a famous television actress or popular male movie star and realize that she or he had weaknesses, faults, and a very real human side. When you think of a famous person, you don't generally visualize him or her naked and entwined with a bunch of other people, but now I did. I had a completely different view. It was the ultimate private party, a closed circle; the Mansion was a place where famous people could do what they wanted and be left alone to do it. A major film actress and her producer husband used to troll the Mansion for girls to bring home. You could wander out to the Jacuzzi at any hour of the day or night and see mini-orgies—tangled-up bodies and arms and limbs. It would be dark and hard to see, and you'd get up closer and say to yourself, *Look what they're doing! My God, what I'm doing isn't so bad!* At some point it really is all relative, depending on where you are and what your environment is. I wasn't judging. I was having fun, though the small-town girl in me came out every once in a while.

I saw everyone I had ever dreamed of meeting at the parties at the Mansion. Bill Cosby was a regular. James Caan, John Belushi,

Dan Ackroyd, Robin Williams, Peter Lawford, Leslie Nielsen, Jack Nicholson, Warren Beatty... each star more famous than the last. All kinds of different, diverse people were in this one space, all focusing on one thing: sex. There would be hundreds of guys hanging out in silk pajamas, plus hundreds of women in their underwear at any of the larger parties. Happy, wild and uninhibited.

It's funny. A lot of people I know from those days have selective lapses of memory. I certainly do! Not to mention that there are a few nights I don't remember at all. The lifestyle at the time—having a butler bring you breakfast at three in the afternoon, if you desired, or dinner at 9am because you were just going to sleep—was truly decadent. I didn't stay naive for long. In fact, I got spoiled pretty quickly. I was wearing the white robe, and I was happy. The white robe was the symbol of acceptance into the inner sanctum; you were going to visit you-know-who. Guests wore colored robes and were confined to the outer perimeters.

Not too long after I had settled into my new lifestyle, my sister Tracy left home and came looking for me. She was the baby, and I had stayed in touch with her. She was just 16 years old when she left home. It was actually supposed to be just a visit to the Mansion, but she arrived, took one look around, and never went back. I had mixed feelings about this; I was torn because I wanted her nearby, of course, but she was only 16. Then again, I remembered what I had been doing when I was that age. But she was a whole different animal. Having had my mother's undivided attention, she was the

ME, TRACY (16 YEARS OLD) AND SISTER SARA.

last to leave home, much more inexperienced and "younger" than I had been at that age. I did my best to keep an eye on her, but I wasn't ready to be a mother figure by any stretch.

Hef and I shared a bedroom just like any regular couple, lounging in bed eating Delmonico steak or melon balls off trays. (He loved melon, but only in balls.) Every afternoon when we woke up Hef's regular breakfast, according to his specifications, would arrive—and now, so did mine. We resided in his huge master suite, which had two stories and its own private video library. We had a wide selection of homemade porno movies for viewing, some of them starring me. People think the tapes Pamela and Paris made were racy...I hope mine never get out!

This inner suite also held all his scrapbooks and archives of his life at the Mansion. Hef did plenty of work there; but needless to say, there was also plenty of play. The master suite was usually open. Though it did have locks, I had a key. Of course there were security cameras all over the Mansion. I've got to hand it to his videographer—Barney is his name—he has seen some stuff he could never repeat in his life. What a job—Hef's videographer. Barney is a very sweet man.

I usually woke up around one or two in the afternoon, depending on how late we'd been up the night before and who had been with us. Hef would head off to his wing of offices to conduct his daily business with the magazine, and I was left to my own devices. First thing I'd run to Tracy's room down the hall and wake her up. She generally stayed up even later than I did, so she was privy to everything that went on after Hef and I went to bed. It was pretty racy stuff for a young girl to see; she got a swift education. Tracy

made friends with the Mansion's social secretaries and butlers and they all had a great time together. When I managed to get up in time, Tracy and I would have our favorite breakfast, the California bagel, then take a swim, see what the other Playmates were doing, and generally come up with some kind of trouble to get into that day.

One of the girls used to lead an aerobics class every afternoon, and Tracy and I would be in there, impossibly hungover, trying to work out. It was crazy; we were both young and naturally thin and didn't really need the exercise, but this was the beginning of the Jane Fonda craze, and we thought it was something we should probably do. We had leg warmers and camel-toe bodysuits, as we called them, because they went so far up the crotch. Life in the Mansion could be like a big slumber party, hanging out with the girls coloring our hair, experimenting with clothes and makeup, getting massages, and pretending to work out.

Some days we'd go out shopping or to visit some friends. It was such a leisurely life that it was a shock to my system. I'd always had jobs since I left school; I was accustomed to being on my own and working hard. Now I had a new car, a place to live, money, free time, and no demands or financial stress. If I wanted to go shopping, Hef would hand over some cash and say, "Have fun." He was a real sugar daddy, in the best sense of the word. Tracy and I had nothing to do but whatever we wanted. Shopping, parties, fun... I was like a kid in a candy store.

I was anxious to drive the Porsche 928 that I had won as

Playmate of the Year. I convinced Hef to come out for a ride with me once, and completely panicked his security team. They were running around with their walkie-talkies saying, "He's off the property! He's off the property!" They came chasing after us as I was driving a hundred miles an hour up Sunset Boulevard. At the time I took him for that wild ride, I imagine Hef hadn't driven himself in years.

We started to prepare for our nightlife at around 5:00 or 6:00 P.M. This was the part I didn't like: acting as hostess to all the people who came to the Mansion. I felt that some of the regulars were abusing Hef's generosity—coming only for the free buffet dinners, movies, and entertainment. Many were longtime friends of his, and I was expected to be nice to them. Their motives didn't bother Hef, because at that point in his life he never wanted to go out or leave the Mansion; he wanted the party to come to him.

Five or six times a year Hef threw huge, elaborate parties. Finding the proper outfit or costume to wear could take weeks. I had my own dressing area in the suite, and half of the huge bathroom, which was bigger than many small houses. For a lingerie party once I had special silk pajamas tailor-made to match his robe. It was all quite decadent.

They were crazy times. A very famous basketball star used to come to see a friend of mine, a beautiful girl who was dating Hef's brother. We'd be hanging out in her bedroom and hear this deep voice coming down the hall: "Debra...Debra..." Then bang, bang, bang on the door—with his penis! We'd be inside cracking up; this

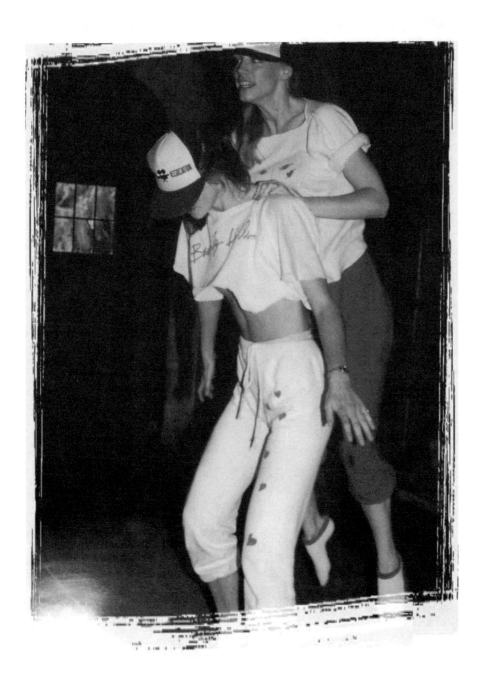

icon was banging on the door with his boner. "This is for you, Debra,"...*thump, thump...* We'd be inside, screaming and laughing.

Sometimes we'd go to Chippendale's, stuff money in the dancers' G-strings, and then bring some of the boys home for a party. Tracy and I used to run around at night, racing through the halls like five-year-olds. Stars like John Belushi would be lounging in the pool with a cocaine bullet stuck in each nostril and beautiful girls all around, and the best-known father figure on TV was offering my teenage sister hash. You never knew what would be going on at any given moment.

*B*reaking *U*p is *H*ard to *D*o

Hugh Hefner was the first famous person I had ever dated. I started at the top and worked sideways, staying right at the top. The world of fame is a different fishbowl. It's both bigger and smaller than you might expect. When you're in the regular world and unknown, certain people are always watching you—the people who mean something to you, like your family and friends—and judging what you do. But when you're dating a famous person, more people, including other well-known people, are all taking note, thinking things like, *Why did he pick her? What's so great about her?*

It's a little bit like Hollywood High. It's competitive in a way, but with really powerful, famous guys, you can't compete for their affections. They like you or they don't. They aren't waiting around to see who does the best splits or cheers. Powerful men pretty much have their choice of women at all times, so they're picking you based on chemistry. And other girls will hate you for it, even if you aren't consciously trying to win over some man.

With Hef, right from the start I thought, *My God. This is a whole different animal. Where he's been, what he's seen, the things that he knows...* My previous boyfriend had been a CFL linebacker, and there wasn't a whole lot of stimulating conversation going on in that relationship. Hef, on the other hand, was fun, intelligent, exciting, boyish, and manly, all at once. He was a whole new package.

It's funny, but with my previous boyfriends the relationships had been much more about sex than those with any of the famous men I dated. Obviously sex is a huge part of any relationship, and it was certainly a big part of mine with Hef. But more important to him at that time was the exclusivity on my part. He is a man who needs a constant primary companion. (And he usually goes for clean-cut, nice girls. Sondra had been a Sunday-school teacher, for heaven's sake.) Of course he had dalliances, but he needed to have one main squeeze. You see this frequently with famous, powerful men. They have the number one girlfriend and a side girlfriend so that if something goes wrong they shouldn't have to, God forbid, go somewhere on their own or be alone for a night.

When the newness of my situation with Hef started to wear off, I started to wonder what else in the world I wanted to do. I had been living in the Mansion for a year, and as wonderful as life was, I had gotten somewhat jaded. The whole thing was getting a tiny bit old. It was no longer all I wanted to do. I started bucking the system a little, not showing up and skipping parties and gatherings. I needed to be by myself sometimes. My inherent work ethic reared its head, and I started saying that I wanted to get a job. I was acting out, because I wasn't able to verbalize what I really wanted. I just knew that what I had was no longer it.

It's not that I didn't know what I had was great, because it was. I felt guilty for even complaining, but the bottom line was that this fabulous lifestyle just wasn't real. It was a fantasy world, and I knew I couldn't live in a fantasy forever. *How long am I going to be the one? How long do I want to do this? How much sex can you have?* As Bill Maher says, "No matter how beautiful a woman is, someone is sick of sleeping with her." I really started bugging Hef about this stuff.

It seemed to me that maybe I could get a job. But, what did I want to do? I had no idea. Hef certainly didn't want me to have a job that would take me away from him. To pacify me, he came up with a job for me at *Playboy on the Scene*, a show that ran on the Playboy Channel, which was then in its infancy. The channel wasn't yet showing pornographic movies. It was trying to be mainstream while maintaining the *Playboy* brand—mainstream, but attractive to a late-night audience. It was an *Entertainment Tonight*-type format featuring adult world news—what strippers do in Russia and so on—from the Playboy point of view. Peter Tomarkin and I were the hosts of the show.

I was thrilled to have a job; it was challenging, especially since I was high all the time when going to work—not good. Someone from Lorimar Studios caught the show and thought I'd be good for a role on *Falcon Crest*, which was then a big nighttime soap on CBS. It was a very small part, but I'd only been in L.A for a year or so and here I was being considered for a role on a prime-time television series. Even if I didn't have many lines, I was lucky. I auditioned and got the part. Believe me, they weren't looking for acting talent. They needed some arm candy, some sexual decoration for the show, and publicized that I was Playmate of the Year and Hugh Hefner's girlfriend. They were trying to boost their audience a little bit, but I don't think I did as much for them as they did for me.

Hef was torn, and so was I. He was happy for me and wanted to be supportive, but he didn't want me to leave. Wasn't there any work I could do here, at home? I had been told to report to work on location in Napa Valley, a date which conflicted with the annual Midsummer Night's Dream party. I said, "I have to go to work, I can't go to the party. It's my new job, I can't stay and be the party hostess with you." I was really chafing at this point. I felt irritated. This relationship was not working out the way I wanted. I was itching for more freedom, even though I knew that the more freedom I took, the faster Hef would replace me. Hugh Hefner is not a man who likes to be single, or alone.

"Look, I really want this job. I'm going to go for it," I told him. But the annual Midsummer Night's Dream party was a big, big deal—the same party where I'd originally met Hef just one year before. He was not about to appear without his girlfriend. When I asked, "How can I be at the party the night before and on the set in Napa Valley the next morning?" Hef replied, "I'll fly you to work." So the party raged all night, and as it was winding down I said, "It's time to go to the airport." My bags were packed and ready to go with me to Napa Valley. My sister, another girl, and I were still partying all the way to the airport. I was wearing, basically, a negligee with a robe over it. I hopped off that plane and went straight into hair and makeup. Talk about making a bad first impression. It doesn't get any worse than that.

It was all over the set. She did what? She flew into work on a private plane? Does she even need this job? I didn't, of course, but I wanted the experience. I'm sure they could see that I was high. I hadn't even slept, and there I was getting my hair and makeup done. Chatting away about the party and who was there, on and on, not even stopping to consider that this was no one else's reality. Everything I said sounded like a complete fabrication.

It didn't even occur to me that this kind of chatter might not endear me to my fellow actors. That they might not really take to me after that. Why wouldn't they like me, I never did anything to them? I just flew in to go to work! In retrospect, my God, I would hate me, too! But there I was and they had to deal with it. David Selby was very sweet and gracious to me; I'm sure he had seen quite a lot in his lifetime. Jane Wyman was there, and Susan Sullivan, who was great. Jane, the former Mrs. Ronald Reagan, couldn't have cared less who I was or how I got there. I saw famous sweater girl Lana Turner, who never did say a word to me. After that inauspicious beginning I had to spend the next few months slowly trying to get into everyone's good graces. I developed a huge crush on David Selby. I didn't do anything about it because he was married, but oh my, he was so cute. There was my wandering eye again...could be a sign of things to come.

I had signed for 10 episodes of *Falcon Crest* and wound up doing 20. In those 20 episodes I probably spoke 20 words—total. E.G. Marshall played my boss. My character was a secretary who was also an insider sent in to sabotage and spy on everyone. It was just a soap, but a pretty popular one at the time. I really had no idea what I was doing, but David was very patient.

THE CAST OF FALCON CREST.

After they finished getting all the exteriors in Napa, the rest of the show was shot on the Warner Bros. lot in L.A. You see it all the time on movies and television—"the lot." It was very exciting to go through the main gate and be greeted by the guard: "Good morning, Miss Tweed!" It was a thrill for me, but I felt a bit of regret, because while I was working, there were some humdingers of parties at my house that I couldn't go to. I knew there were girls circling Hef, thinking, *She's gone, this is my chance to move in.* The tension in the air was palpable. I could feel other girls nipping at my heels.

Hef could have said, "Come on home, and we'll go on like we were. You don't have to work." I sensed that he wanted to say that, and I was very conflicted. In a way I was done with that life, and wanted to do everything on my own...but not really. What I really wanted was to be with him, my way, and that wasn't going to happen.

I found an agent, John Larocca, who once represented Michelle Pfeiffer when she was starting out. He sent me around on some auditions, but it was a tough sell. I was six feet tall and known only as a Playmate. There just weren't that many roles that were right for me, even though by now I was growing into and developing "my look" and actually starting to believe in myself. I realized that while I may not have had outstanding talent, I wasn't a bad actress.

I was offered a movie role after my work on the series ended, for a picture starring Peter Weller that was shooting in Canada. I must admit that the Canadian content laws really helped me get that role. Many Canadian actors were coming to L.A. in the eighties to further their acting careers, only to be booked on gigs back home, because Canada offered rebates and tax incentives to use local talent.

Back at the Mansion there was great dissension in the ranks. I was on my way to Canada, hearing all this gossip about girls going in and out of Hef's room, and I was pissed. It wasn't the jealous, "I love him, how can he do this to me" kind of pissed. It was more the "Why can't I have everything?" kind of pissed. But you just can't have everything. I decided to get back at him by having an affair with Peter Weller, whom I met on the airplane flying to location to Montreal. We made out in the first class section for most of the trip. It was my first real "cheat" on Hef, since technically he and I were still living together. Peter was also my first taste of leading-man syndrome: falling in love with your leading man for a nanosecond. On the set, romances last for as long as the movie. When it's over, you wind up asking yourself, *What did I see in him anyway? He was pretty good-looking on the set, because he was the big cheese.* Then once the picture wraps, you're kind of done with him.

When we got back in town after the movie wrapped, Peter wanted to see the Mansion, so I invited him to one of the parties. I was still Hef's official girlfriend, but since I had heard from the butlers that Hef had not been wasting his time either, I was a little mad at him. It wasn't that I wanted him to ask my permission—we weren't monogamous in the traditional sense—but I felt a little cheated on. I had heard from several people that a girlfriend of mine had been hitting on Hef from the moment I left. Payback's a bitch! My friend, who would later become quite a famous TV personality, wanted to be in *Playboy* in the worst way; she used to cry on my shoulder about it all the time. (Even after her fling with Hef, she still didn't get in. Ironically, *Playboy* wanted to put her in the magazine after she got famous, but by then she was done with them.) I realized it was time to move into my own apartment in L.A., so my sister and a girlfriend, Cindy, who was dating Hef's son David, and I rented a place—one I never stayed in until we broke up, but it was there, ready. I was at the "just in case" stage, waiting for the inevitable.

The night Peter Weller showed up at the Mansion pretty much spelled the end of Hef's and my relationship. Peter had a great time, but I was just not into the whole Mansion party scene anymore. I'd had a little taste of independence, and I wanted to see where it took me, but I still wanted everything; I was confused again. Twenty-five years old and at another major crossroad. By the end of the evening I'd made up my mind to meet Peter at his hotel later. We'd been spending every night together while shooting the movie. My sister, who had missed me while I was away, rode with me in the Porsche to our apartment. She was always up for some adventure, and now happily came along for the ride. She said, "Shannon, I think we're being followed." I laughed it off, but she said, "No, really. We're being followed."

I started dodging and weaving, going in and out of side streets like we were in some kind of movie. I don't know what I was thinking... that I could lose them? Not likely. It was so silly. We made it to my apartment, where I showered and packed an overnight bag. I figured whoever was following us would be gone by then, so I took off for the Beverly Wilshire Hotel, where Peter was staying, and didn't think any more about it. The next morning, as I was coming through the lobby, I saw one of Hef's security guys standing by the front doors, waiting for me. I just said, "Oh, good morning." That was pretty much the end of that relationship. It was clearly not working out for either one of us.

Hef was a great boyfriend. He was always loving and supportive, but hey, he wanted a girlfriend with him at home. He wanted what he wanted; I wanted what I wanted. There was no terrible, bitter breakup—nothing traumatic at all. It was a chapter in both our lives that was over. I wasn't going to cry about it. Well, not much. I think a huge mistake many women make is to think, *Okay, I've found the guy, and now I'm going to change him.* Women find a guy and try to change him, but he never does; men find a woman and hope she won't ever change, and she always does. As a woman, to hope you will change a man—that's a fool's game. Hef wasn't going to change for me. There wasn't going to be any more compromise on either side.

During our year and a half together Hef had given me many fabulous gifts—but especially confidence in myself. He made me feel tremendously important and valued. He treated me like an adult and asked my opinion about things, engaged me in conversation, and never treated me like a doll. I owe him big. He did a great deal

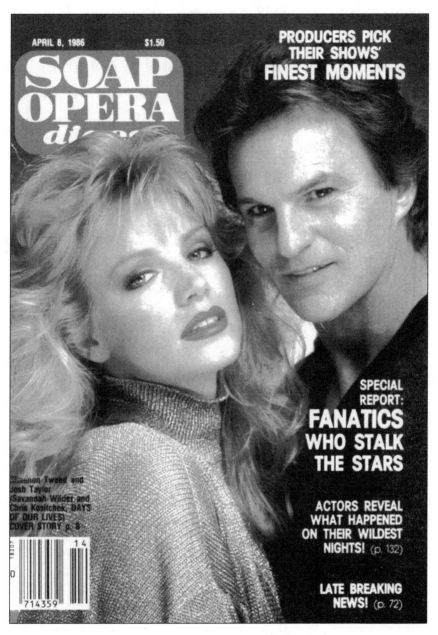

JOSH TAYLOR PLAYED MY LOVE INTEREST ON DAYS OF OUR LIVES. WE HAD
FUN TOGETHER, AND WERE AMONG THE FIRST TO START MAKING OUT IN
STRANGE PLACES (I.E. ON THE BAR) ON DAYTIME SOAPS.

for me: for my sense of self, for my finances, and I would even say for my sense of morality, though that's certainly quite subjective! He even supported me through our breakup: He paid my rent and gave me Louis XIV furniture for my little apartment. We split the dogs we both loved and stayed in touch. We remained friends; I missed him a lot, and I visited him frequently.

I landed a job as a regular on a soap, *Days of our Lives*, and things calmed down a little. I was on my own, for real this time.

CHAPTER SEVEN

Sexy in the City

Shortly after I moved in with Tracy and Cindy, my sister and I decided to move into a different apartment on our own. We found a place on Burton Way in Beverly Hills, where we lived next door to George Hamilton. In addition to the role on *Days of Our Lives*, I started getting a lot of work guest-starring on shows like *Fantasy Island*. I still saw Hef pretty regularly, while attending screenings and parties at the Mansion, and he continued to help me with all sorts of things, depending on how I was doing. Sometimes I was lonely and missed him. Soon after our breakup, he acquired a new girlfriend, the polar opposite of me. She was pretty, with dark hair and eyes, and rumored to be unstable and a little wacky. Well, maybe not *that* opposite of me! They had a tumultuous relationship, which was evident later in a palimony suit brought by her against Hef. As for me, I never saw Peter again after leaving the Beverly Wilshire that morning. I was done with that, too. The set romance was over.

I was enjoying my freedom. It was the early eighties in L.A. and everybody was on some kind of drug. So many people were doing cocaine back then, you couldn't find anybody sober. Even the casting agents were high. I was running around town, burning through my money, buying friends left and right. I had a few casual dates during this time, and a few strange ones, too, including a five-week relationship with producer Robert Evans, though I don't think he even remembers it! I barely do. He was debonair and charming, and I remember he wanted me to dress differently and gave me his silk shirts to wear. I think he did that with every girl after Ali McGraw! Odd, but—whatever. He was a fun distraction for a little while.

Around this time, 1983, I went off to shoot a film, *Hot Dog... The Movie*. It was really a great little cult movie, very popular when it was released. Part of its appeal might have been that you could see everyone's breasts, but probably more important were the Olympic-caliber ski doubles that were featured. Everybody thought the skiing sequences were so authentic; we were all very into the sport part of it. *Hot Dog* marked my first time appearing naked in a movie. It was a very strange experience.

I was not anxious to appear totally nude. If the audience could catch a glimpse while I walked by onscreen, that was one thing, but I didn't want to do the Annette Bening number where you just stand there naked talking for a few minutes—remember *The Grifters?* I just wasn't that brave yet. First of all, *Hot Dog* wasn't a high-enough quality film. The funny thing is, the bigger the movie, the more willing most actresses are to run around naked. That's interesting, because a higher-quality, bigger-budget movie draws more people to see it, and therefore more people see you naked. As an actress in a low-budget film, you debate, *Hmmm, I don't know if I want to show my tits, it's not a very good movie.* But *Hot Dog* was the best role I was offered at the time. When you're at that stage, you just try to be the best actor in the project. I was going to do a good job and not worry about the writing and the plot and all that. I was just a peon.

So, there I was in the hot tub with my costar, shooting my first nude love scene, and there was a problem: he kept getting an erection, which the director kept seeing emerge above water. I was taken aside and told, "Look Shannon, you've got to help us out, because we have to keep shooting this over because we keep getting a glimpse of his thing." Immediately I shot back, "Oh, you can see my thing but not his thing, that's how it works?" But that *is* the way it works, so I just used my elbow to keep it down underwater. I'm not sure my costar knew what we were doing, though I'm sure he will now. In the end, only my breasts showed while we were fake-humping. Except in water scenes, I always wore my merkin. Some actors called it a "Barbie patch" because it was usually a nude-colored triangle of fabric taped over the pubic area. Men wore a kind of sock, if you will.

Everything in love scenes is fake, and that's odd, because the only experience that would be helpful for the scene is really making out with the other person. So when it came to kissing the other actor, I wasn't sure what I should do. Give him tongue, or not? *Is he supposed to be doing this? Is he taking advantage of me? How can he be getting a boner; isn't this atmosphere too nerve-racking for that to happen?* Apparently not. Since that first time I've done plenty of love scenes, and, even when you don't really get along with the man you're doing a scene with, I'm here to tell you that guys are dogs, they'll get it up for anybody. If a guy ever tells you he can't get it up because he has a headache or something, take it from me, he's lying. A man can be in a fake love scene surrounded by crew members making out with a woman he doesn't even like, and he'll get it up. It's just an automatic push-button response. But, just for the record, every love scene I ever did on film was simulated. There was no soft porn, no sex whatsoever.

There were always plenty of guys on the crew standing around, but they were mostly used to seeing love scenes and naked girls. I didn't mind too much, because everyone had pretty much seen me naked before—I had been in *Playboy*, after all. But it was different moving around nude. I always made sure to have a good relationship with the lighting guy and the cameraman, because in the end they were very important to me. "If you light the cheese on the back of my leg, I will hunt you down and kill you!"—that type of thing. It's important to get a good rapport going with the crew, and I always did. We got along famously.

On the *Hot Dog* set one particular guy on the crew caught my eye immediately; he could have been a Burt Reynolds double. I really liked him, and he really liked me, so it was full speed ahead. I wanted to have some fun, and we started to have an affair on location at Lake Tahoe. This new guy was so-o-o cute, but something was not quite right. I just couldn't put my finger on exactly what it was.

When the movie wrapped we both returned to L.A. and carried on with the affair. I gave him a key to my apartment on Burton Way. One night I came home to find him wearing women's clothes. My first thought was, "Wow, you make a really ugly chick." What I said was, "My God, where do you go dressed up like that. What do you do?"

Obviously I am not a person who sees something and gets totally uptight and appalled by it or runs away. I go there. *What is this thing that you like? Let me check it out and see.* That's always been my attitude. If curiosity killed the cat, at least four of my lives must be used up by now. And in the end, sex wasn't much different, just better for him.

He took me to the Queen Mary, a club where they performed drag shows. Obviously, I was not thinking straight, because once we got there everybody immediately knew who I was. I had a following, and not only that, it turned out I was wildly popular with cross dressers. I thought, "Oh God, what have I done? I've been outed or something." It was very strange to be recognized, to have people come up to me and want to meet me. I learned that there were actually drag queens who wanted to be me. They knew who I was. They're attracted to strong women, and being six feet tall made me quite an imposing presence. I stood there in the drag club thinking, "What an odd fan base."

The drag queens were amazingly talented. It was unbelievable how they sang more like Diana Ross and Cher than the real thing. So my boyfriend and I went there a few times, but the novelty quickly wore off for me. I started looking around for new dates. A cross-dresser wasn't quite the ideal boyfriend material I had in mind.

A few weeks later I started seeing producer Joel Silver, a filmmaker who's well known for his big blockbuster films. I met him at some movie or fight night at the Mansion. Joel was a vivacious workaholic with a quick wit—all traits I admired. His business partner, Jimmy Iovine, was seeing another Playmate named Vicki. They went on to get married and have four children, and she later became an author, writing a hip guide to motherhood.

I remember walking in Las Vegas once when Joel turned to me and asked, "Why can't you be more like Vicki?" She was a preppy little brunette, and we couldn't have been more different in looks or temperament. She's a great girl, but his comment bothered me. "Joel, why are you dating me if you want me to be more like Vicki?" I was still looking for the right man, and he certainly hadn't found his ideal girl in me.

One night Joel and I were sitting around his house when we both heard an anguished cry: "I hope you're happy now!" Then—*tap, tap, tap*—the sound of high heels running away down the driveway. We jumped up to see who it was, and it was my cross-dresser, wearing his high heels. He had been peeking through the windows, spying on me! He had followed me. He was brokenhearted because he thought I was cheating on him, but in my mind what we had was

GREGORY HARRISON

not what I considered a relationship. He was married, for God's sake, and cheating on his wife in a dress! To this day Joel still tells that "I hope you're happy now!" story. So embarrassing.

Somewhere around this time I worked as a guest star on a television show, and while I was on the lot I ran into Gregory Harrison, who was starring in *Trapper John, M.D.* We had a little liaison. One day he said, "I'm going to go surfing, do you want to come?" I said sure, and off we went with friends to Australia. Somehow his wife, whom he had forgotten to tell me about, found out about this, and called to tell him: "Your shit's on the driveway." This was back when actors never told anyone they were married, because then they wouldn't be considered "hot." The surf date was suddenly over; he raced back to L.A. because he didn't want to lose half his stuff, and he's stayed with his wife to this day, as far as I know. Ah, the power of alimony.

I was batting a thousand at this point and figured I was going to have to start asking "Are you married?" It was quite an active little year or two; I was feeling my oats, having fun. I had some good taste, I had some bad taste, but I was tasting. I had some good judgment, I had some bad judgment, but I never made judgments. "Equal opportunity for all" was my motto. It was great, but I hadn't fallen in love with anybody, though not for lack of looking. My career was plodding along, but not really shooting up.

Our huge apartment next door to George Hamilton was really too big for just my sister and me. It was also too expensive. I was making good money acting, but my sister and I were going through every dime I brought in. Tracy was dabbling in modeling a bit by now and was leading her own separate life, meeting and hanging out with all kinds of people. She met Chico Ross, Diana Ross's little brother, through a mutual friend named Ruben, and they dated for a while. On a whim the two of them eloped to Vegas. Tracy told my mom about the wedding by phone but was too afraid to tell me. She thought that I would talk her out of it—I might have tried.

It's possible that Tracy and Chico felt a bond because they both had famous sisters, the second-banana kind of feeling. To me, Tracy was never a second banana. In fact, I had always wanted to be like her. She was so cute, smart and athletic that people were always attracted to her instantly; she never even had to try. She was just so likeable, everything I wanted to be and thought I wasn't. I wanted my sister to be happy and forgave her for not telling me about the wedding. It wasn't like it changed our lifestyle; she and Chico never really lived separately from me for even one day. For a wedding present I gave them my Mazda 626, the one I'd bought in my Toronto days. Chico lost it. Don't ask me how you lose a car, but that kind of behavior pretty much sums Chico up at that point in time.

Ruben, not Chico, became our roommate in a new apartment on Doheny Drive in West Hollywood. So, along with Tracy, Chico, Ruben, and all my new girlfriends, the party continued. But the yearly Midsummer Night's Dream party was coming up, and it would soon change my life yet again.

💋   💋   💋

On my original Playmate data sheet, an embarrassing handwritten list of my favorite things that accompanied my layout, I had written down Tom Selleck as someone I liked, hoping he might read it. He did. (This was long before he met and married his wife.) We began chatting on the phone every now and then, trying to set a date to get together. When the annual Midsummer Night's Dream party at the Playboy Mansion was coming up, he was off working on a movie in Vancouver with Gene Simmons and Kirstie Alley.

Tracy was surprised that I didn't want to go to the party that year, but I was really tired of the dating scene and all the guys who said they were single and turned out to be married. I was also tired of the guys who were only interested in dating me because I had been Hef's girlfriend and all the expectations that came along with it. Finally Tracy talked me into accompanying her. We dressed in our usual Mansion party fashion, that is to say, we were basically wearing butt floss. This was at the height of the Madonna craze, and we looked the part.

When we arrived we saw a music producer, Richard Perry, who was friends with both of us. We all stood together chatting for a while, and the name Gene Simmons came up. Tracy knew who Gene Simmons was, but I wasn't very familiar with KISS. The clubs in which I worked had booked acts like the Commodores, the Spinners, and Tom Jones (my favorite). I loved Motown, so I didn't know of Gene at all. Of course I'd heard the "Beth" song on the radio a million times along with everyone else, but I certainly didn't know who he was by sight.

Gene had wrapped his acting role in *Runaway* before Tom finished, and a couple of girls brought him to the Midsummer Night's Dream party. When Tracy spotted him she said, "You've got to meet this guy." I was thinking, *That's all I need. Another womanizer.* Tracy said, "Come on, he's really nice, really smart; you'll see. And he has a job!" Richard said, "Yes, she's right." Now, of course, they both take credit for introducing us. It was a joint effort. They both walked me over to introduce me to Gene Simmons.

Gene had short hair for his movie role and was wearing white silk pajamas—only pajamas. He looked a little shiny, a little shady, with slicked-back hair and a cocky grin. It became very clear that he wasn't wearing underwear the longer we spoke. I was standing there doing my best aloof Madonna imitation in a white lace bathing suit, white lace bobby socks, black high-heeled pumps, and a little black lace overcoat that didn't close. I was virtually naked. And I had big eighties hair, frizzed out to here. Tons of makeup. My look was up-to-the-minute at the time, but my God, when I see photos, I wish I had never taken one picture throughout the entire decade. Such a hideous era—even worse than the seventies. But clearly Gene thought I was looking pretty good.

I can't say that it was love at first sight, at least not for me. He immediately went into his whole Gene routine. I was not impressed. My main thought was, *Oh God. A musician.* He was just talking on and on like he does, and I was just standing there thinking, *Not a hope in hell pal, but keep on talking.* He was tap-dancing, singing, telling jokes—doing anything he could think of to get my attention. Meanwhile I did the Hollywood thing, where you look over the person's shoulder to see who else is around.

I listened for a few minutes and was ready to go. "Excuse me," I broke in, "It was nice to meet you," and walked away. He was a little surprised by that. He wasn't used to girls not liking him as much as he liked them. I was done; I didn't give him another thought. As we were walking away Tracy said, "Don't you know who that was?" I said, "Umm, a musician I think he was saying?" Tracy said, "Come on, you know the song, "I wanna rock and roll all nite, and party every day." And I replied, "Well, kind of, I guess I've heard it on the radio, a long time ago, but what has he done lately?" Tracy just looked at me. She explained to me that KISS was still going strong, and described the makeup and the whole deal. I just said, "Okay, fine." I still wasn't particularly interested.

As the night wore on, my sister and I were downing B-52s and running around having a fine time. Hours later we were just about ready to call it a night when we came out of a bathroom and saw Gene standing there, bent over examining a Dali or some piece of art on the wall. I don't know what possessed me—probably the booze—but I yelled out, "Hey, nice ass!" So classy, don't you think? It was an impulse; the words just flew out of my mouth. I had slammed the door shut earlier, but opened it up a tiny crack, just for the hell of it. He came right back over with the whole song and dance. He was really trying hard; it was cute and it endeared him to me. Once you blow them off, guys usually just skulk off with their heads down, but not Gene. He had great self-confidence. Earlier Tracy had filled me in some more about KISS, and seeing his attitude, I thought, *Hey, why not, I'll give it a try.* We started talking again, and he started listening. That's where he won me over. Tracy disappeared.

Gene is so smart, and bright, and funny, and he was really trying hard to impress me. He was working at it, and it touched me. The only problem was, I was drunk. We were talking about all kinds of things. I'm sure he went through his whole litany about no smoking, no drugs, a clean life—all that. I forgot every word he said and took him down to the wine cellar. (Remember, I used to live in the Mansion, so I knew where all the secret buttons and passages were.) I tried to focus and maintain a little dignity as I was going down the basement stairs thinking, "Okay, if I fall down

MISS NOVEMBER 1981.

LOOK AT WHAT A COUPLE OF YOUNG WHIPPERSNAPPERS WE WERE! WITH HEF AT ONE OF THE MANY MANSION PARTIES.

STEVE GARVEY AND LEROY NEIMAN. DOESN'T HEF LOOK GREAT HERE?

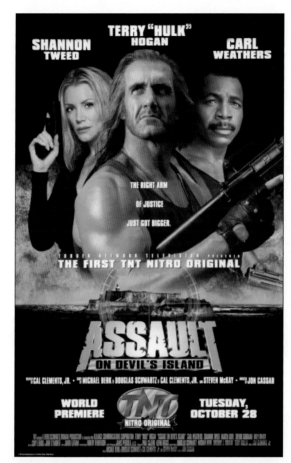

I LOVED WORKING ON THESE MOVIES WITH HULK HOGAN. IT WAS NICE TO BE RUNNING AND FIGHTING FOR A CHANGE. THIS FILM AND ITS SEQUEL WERE PRODUCED BY THE PEOPLE THAT BRING YOU BAYWATCH, WHICH I ALSO GUEST-STARRED ON.

A COMEDY STARRING BILL MAHER.

IF IT CAN'T SCARE
THEM TO DEATH
IT WILL FIND
ANOTHER WAY.

OF
UNKNOWN
ORIGIN

MY FIRST MOVIE WITH PETER WELLER.

A FEW OF THE MANY STRAIGHT-TO-
VIDEO OR TELEVISION MOVIES I'VE HAD
THE PLEASURE OF WORKING ON.

WITH MICHAEL PARE – HE WAS SUCH A
CUTIE!

THAT'S ME IN PINK IN MY SECOND
FILM – I NEVER SKIED AN INCH.

ANDREW AND I DID NIGHT EYES II, III AND IV.

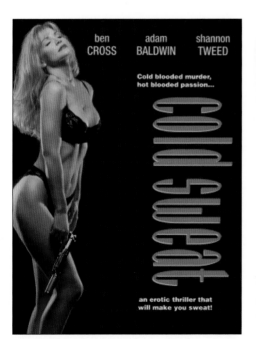

PLAYBOY

ENTERTAINMENT FOR MEN

JUNE 1982 • $2.50

Playmate of the Year

FOR A LONGER LOOK AT SHANNON TWEED,
OPEN THIS GATEFOLD COVER,
THEN TURN TO HER FABULOUS PICTORIAL INSIDE

THE FEMINIST LOBBY: WHAT ELSE DO WOMEN WANT?

PLAYBOY

ENTERTAINMENT FOR MEN

MARCH 1982 • $3.00

PLAYBOY INTERVIEW
**What Makes
60 MINUTES
Tick?**

HOW TO SAVE
CARL LEWIS
FROM HIMSELF

**12 DREAMY
PAGES OF
PLAYMATES
OF THE YEAR
UNDRESSED
FOR BED**

PLAYBOY

ENTERTAINMENT FOR MEN

JANUARY 1998 • $5.95

HOLIDAY
ANNIVERSARY
ISSUE

**COVER GIRL
SHANNON
TWEED**

QUEEN OF THE B's
GOES PRIME TIME

GRANT HILL
INTERVIEW

SLING BABE
BILLY BOB
THORNTON'S
OUTRAGEOUS EX

BETTIE PAGE
"MY STORY"

A YEAR-IN-SEX
TO DIE FOR

TERI HATCHER
20 QUESTIONS

HOW SMART ARE YOU
ABOUT SEINFELD?

HIP HOP
CAN IT STEP
OUT FROM ITS
GANGSTA PAST?

SHEL SILVERSTEIN'S
STREET SMART
HAMLET

PLUS THE 1997
PLAYMATE REVIEW
NEW FICTION FROM
ARTHUR C. CLARKE
BRUCE JAY FRIEDMAN
AND TOM PAINE

GREAT NEW YEAR'S
HIGH-JINKS AND A
WHOLE LOT MORE

PLAYBOY

ENTERTAINMENT FOR MEN

MAY 1986 • $3.50

**VICTORIA
SELLERS**

PETER'S
DAUGHTER IS A
PHOTOGRAPHIC
CHIP OFF THE
OLD BLOCK

LINDA ELLERBEE
ON LIFE INSIDE
THE TUBE

"FATAL
VISION"
REVISITED

GREEN BERET
DOCTOR JEFFREY
MACDONALD
INTERVIEWED

STALLONE VS.
SPRINGSTEEN!
WHICH ONE'S THE
WORKING-CLASS
HERO?

THE MERRY
MORTICIAN

A HARD-TO-BELIEVE
NUDE PICTORIAL

WITH MY SISTER TRACY

PLAYBOY

Celebrity
CENTERFOLD

SHANNON TWEED

TEST SHOTS FOR THE VIDEO
BOX COVER FOR PLAYBOY.

Mischievous.   Bold.   Fun.

Sexy.   Want more?

PLAYBOY's
Celebrity Centerfold

SHANNON TWEED

AVAILABLE NOVEMBER 19, 1996

A DREAMY WATERCOLOR BY OLIVIA.

EVEN PHOTOGRAPHERS TYPECAST ME IN THIS GLAMOROUS WAY.

THANK YOU.

HI!

THESE ARE PICTURES SO MEN
WILL BUY MY BOOK!

Mother's Day.

Going to the Easter egg hunt at the Playboy mansion.

DOESN'T EVERY FAMILY HAVE A SHOT LIKE THIS?

ON OUR WAY TO HEF'S NEW YEAR'S EVE PARTY.

ONE BIG, HAPPY FAMILY.

these stairs that will be the end of this one." I had been single for a while now and it was nice to meet someone I had chemistry with who was also single, or so I thought.

I made it down the stairs—barely. The whole time he was talking away, talking away, and I wasn't hearing a word he said. So I just laid a kiss on him. Made a big pass at him. I was fully prepared to make out hot and heavy right there. And I have to say, when I kissed him, I was like *What the hell was that??* It was the biggest tongue I'd ever felt in my life. Despite the shock, however, I was ready to go, but he wouldn't! *Gene Simmons wouldn't!* Later he told me I wasn't some groupie who was going to give him a blow job and walk away. It wasn't going to be like that. All I was thinking was, *Okay, you're cute, I'll do ya.* I was coming off a pretty wild life, so this encounter wasn't a big deal to me. But he wasn't going to cooperate. Gene was saying, "Okay, we'd better go." I'm thinking, *You've got me alone in a wine cellar and you want to go? Well, okay; fine.* I was a little taken aback. This was not the way it usually went.

He said, "Look, let's go out tomorrow."

I said, "I can't, I'm going away tomorrow to do a movie in Toronto; I'll be there a few weeks." I had a little part in one of the *Meatballs* sequels, not a big step up for my career, or at all, really.

He didn't give up. "Here's what I'll do, I'll come over in the morning for breakfast before you leave. I'll bring you caviar and champagne and the whole thing. We'll have a nice breakfast before you go."

I was still surprised he wouldn't make out with me. I just said "Okay, sure. My flight's at 11, come over before 10 or I'll be gone."

RECENT PHOTO BY RICHARD FEGELY FOR PLAYBOY.

Even though I was pretty tipsy, I could feel that something was different about this guy.

That's why I was surprised when the next morning came and he didn't call or show up. I was pissed off. Tracy went over to the Beverly Hills Hotel, where Gene had said he was staying, with a picture of me while I packed. On the back of the photo I had written, "If you really do have the balls you say you have maybe you'll call me sometime." I put my phone number on it again for good measure. For all I knew he'd been looped, too, and just forgot.

Gene called immediately to say, "You gave me the wrong number last night." I said, "You liar, I did not." He said he was coming right over and we were going to have breakfast and champagne and all that.

When Gene showed up, my roommate Ruben was just leaving. That got Gene's attention: one guy was walking out just as he was walking in. The first thing he did was hand me the note I had written my number on the night before, and sure enough, I had given him the number I used when I didn't want people to call me. I would just change the last digit. I had done it so many times that I didn't realize it. He just looked at me and said, "Wrong number." Gene had been calling the poor guy with the other number all morning saying, "Look, if you're the husband or the boyfriend and you don't want me to talk to her, just say so. She gave me this number to call and I'm calling." He really tried, God love him. What could I say but, "Sorry, sorry, oops, sorry."

I was expecting a lavish meal, and here he just wanted to show me that note with the wrong number. I said, "Gotta go. Heading to the airport. Nice seeing you again. Thanks for that breakfast you didn't bring." He said, "I will send my driver for breakfast right now." I said, "You have a *driver*? Where's your car?" He said, "I don't drive." I cracked up. I've been driving since I was twelve, tractors and everything. This was L.A. for God's sake. Everybody drove.

When I asked, "Why don't you drive?" Gene said he was from New York and had never needed to learn; he took taxis or subways. He added, "Look, I'll send the driver right now to pick up some breakfast from Greenblatt's." It was at that point he realized he had forgotten his wallet. I could not believe this guy. All I could say was, "You are the biggest loser. You are a *loser*, and I've got to run now. Bye-bye."

He did a strange thing as I was leaving. Gene pulled my sweater out from the waistband and stuck his head completely up and under my sweater. It was so weird, it was almost enough to make me say bye-bye for good, but then he came back up and gave me a great kiss. He told me, "I'm going to call you every day." I said, "Oh sure you are," and headed out the door shaking my head.

But he did call me every day while I was in Canada. And he's called me every day since then, for the past 22 years.

CHAPTER EIGHT

Beauty and the Beast

To find someone who truly adores you is the greatest thing in the world. I had been looking for such a long time for something, and I found it in Gene. I'm sure it was more than just one thing; it was a combination of many of his qualities. But it was also that waiting-to-exhale thing. With Gene, I could finally just breathe normally, and it was a great feeling. I don't think Gene knew what was going to happen when we met; I certainly didn't. I think he immediately sensed I was someone special, otherwise he would have made a move on me in the wine cellar. Something in him told him right from the start not to treat this like a quickie.

Gene and I talked every day while I was in Canada and decided that I would fly directly from Toronto to visit him in New York. I had only spent a couple of hours at the party with him, then a few minutes the next morning when he came by to visit. Since then we'd had some great conversations and I was excited to see him again, but truly, I didn't know what to expect.

When the shoot ended I flew directly to New York. He was waiting, and the whole scene was straight off the cover of a romance novel, with Gene as the hero. Flowers, a limousine, food—we headed straight for his place. I didn't leave New York for three months! I stayed for so long that Tracy eventually had to fly in and bring me my dog, Vanilla. Tracy stayed for a while, then took off for Europe to model.

While I was in Canada, I had heard a few things about Mr. Simmons. For one thing, I knew from Tracy that he had something going on with Diana Ross. Just a few days after I arrived Gene picked up the phone and called Diana Ross and told her, "Look, I've met somebody, and I don't want you to read about it in the tabloids or anything. But I've met this girl Shannon and I want to spend some time with her." I was impressed with his honesty and forthrightness. He didn't have to do that. He could have avoided an uncomfortable discussion for a long time.

Gene really won my heart; he tried so hard. He placed candles around the bathtub, he brought me scones and jam and tea in bed, and food whenever I was hungry. As anyone who knew Gene then or knows him now can attest, this behavior was completely out of character for him. The man can barely make a sandwich. He was knocking himself out, though I didn't fully appreciate what an effort this was for him. Several of his previous girlfriends had had housekeepers and chefs. I thought I must certainly be the poorest girlfriend he'd had in quite a while; he actually had to do things for me. The whole dynamic of our relationship was very new to him, but he liked doing things for me, and it was very endearing. He actually picked his clothes up off the floor while I was there—something he hasn't done since. He wanted to make a good impression, and I wanted him to want me around.

Gene was different from the other guys I'd been with, because he was so completely accepting of me. I didn't ever have to be embarrassed about opening up too much…. or think, "Oh, if I say that he's got ammo." I'd had those thoughts with other people. And it was just not like that with Gene. I was still smoking cigarettes at the time, a habit he just hated, but he didn't give me any grief about it. It wasn't a deal breaker. Nothing I did was a deal breaker. I was the exception to all his rules. I suddenly had a man who just wanted to make me happy. He'd head out to rehearse and come home and I'd still be in bed! He'd just happily jump back in. It was so romantic, I couldn't believe it. I thought, *This, too, has to pass. Another not-real situation. Too good to be true.* But it wasn't.

One day Gene took me to Bloomingdale's for a shopping spree. Hef had given me presents sometimes, but let's face it, I knew his secretary had been the one who picked them out. The sentiment had been there; Hef was thoughtful and I appreciated it when he said something like "Go out and buy yourself a dress," but I had never experienced anything like this shopping trip with Gene.

Not knowing New York, I'd never been inside Bloomingdale's.

We walked around the store and Gene said, "Pick out whatever you want." He sat patiently while I modeled all the latest fashions. I had certainly never shopped on this scale—one with an unlimited budget. I was in heaven in the Donna Karan section, trying on everything I could put my hands on, while Gene said to sales staff, "She'll take that. And that. And that." Coats and hats and thigh-high boots. Sweaters and accessories and outfits. Gene was helping me try on a gigantic Donna Karan rhinestone belt, very fashionable and trendy at the time, when security approached me and asked if everything was all right, because Gene looked like a thug. "It's all right, he's with me—not to mention he's paying!" I told them. (I still have that belt, by the way, up in my closet. I can't buckle it around my waist anymore, but we won't talk about that.) So then Gene found a personal shopper to come assist me—as if I needed any help. I've never needed help spending money, only making it.

The whole thing was just fabulous. I needed some new clothes, because all I had with me was what I brought in my suitcase from the Toronto shoot, but this was way beyond anything I could have imagined. I'm not sure he was thinking clearly, because Gene was setting quite a standard, one that he would never want to live up to again, ever. Trust me on that one.

We were having so much fun. I loved New York, its pace and rhythms were perfect for me. It was certainly more of a city like Toronto than L.A. was, with busy sidewalks and high-rises and crowds of people walking everywhere. We'd go out to dinner and order two of every dessert and try them all. We went to the Russian

Tea Room one evening and ordered the entire dessert cart. The whole pastry thing was new to me; I developed quite a sugar habit in New York. My feelings for Gene grew stronger every day. I had found someone who would finally put me up on my own little pedestal like my dad had. It was incredible to have that feeling of being cherished once more. Any defenses I had crumbled; the feeling really grew into love. When I was ready to give back, Gene was right there waiting.

I met the other members of KISS on that trip. Paul was handsome and charismatic, but I knew he had seen girls come and go. I wanted to make a good impression on him, because I knew Gene loved him and respected his opinion. Eric Carr was with the band then; what a sweet guy he was. I ventured out a couple of times to watch Gene rehearse and see what KISS was all about. He actually got a little shy playing in front of me. He was blushing. They had to practice where each band member would walk during each song so they wouldn't crash into each other, and I watched them map out their territory. This was just practice; no fire breathing, no costumes, no bombs going off. It looked funny, and I had to giggle, watching him scuttle around the stage.

Gene had made me aware of his feelings about drinking and drug use right from the start. "Drinking is for losers," is certainly something he said to me on more than one occasion. I said, "Gene, we're not all losers just because we have a drink. I will agree with you that it's not especially good for you. I have a lot of vices that I'm probably willing to give up for the right reasons, when I'm ready. And when I'm ready, I'll let you know." I was being cocky, but I knew that if I didn't give these things up, I wouldn't be able to have a serious relationship with him.

Alcohol and drugs were not going to fly in Gene's world, but I think I'd been looking for a reason to quit all that. I'd been partying hard for years, and I was tired; I was pretty much done. It was time to grow up and be sober. I felt for the first time I was entering a healthy environment, becoming one-half of a healthy relationship. It was good for me and good for him.

Nothing changed overnight. I continued to drink for a while, but not get drunk. The night I met Gene was the last of its kind. If we were out for dinner and I ordered a drink, he wouldn't confront me about it. He was still trying to make a good impression on me, of course, and was on his best behavior. He would just sit there and wait—like something was going to happen. I would say, "You've been around enough drunks to know that nothing happens when you have one drink. Don't sit there and act like because I have a glass of champagne I'm going to fall off my chair and cause a scene." But Gene likes to drive his points home. He beats things to death. I got the message.

I did eventually quit drinking, but not because he objected. I had been drinking for so long to help me cope or help me be less shy or for whatever reason, and it was something I just didn't need anymore. I didn't miss it. It's no fun to drink alone, and now I had a guy who was as clean and sober as it gets. Mr. Goody Two-shoes, Dudley Do-Right.

Those months I spent with Gene were a dry-out spell. The whole New York experience was wonderful, and our relationship was still too good to be true. But I had to get back to work, and life had to go back to a new normal. It was time to incorporate my family, my life, and my work into our new world. When I got home to L.A., all my friends were still running around doing this and doing that. Gene went on tour and I was alone, so I fell back into the party life a little bit. And the funny thing was, it wasn't so great. I looked around and thought, *All this isn't as fun as I remember.* I just didn't want to do it anymore.

A few months after I returned to L.A. I headed off to Africa to do a movie. I was traveling all over the place; so was Gene. No matter where either of us was in the world, Gene faithfully called me every single day. Slowly I dropped the friends who were still doing drugs and all those things I didn't want to do anymore. I think that should be Step One of any 12-step program: Get away from it. Get away from the people around you doing that kind of stuff, it's half the battle. I think I was lucky, because I had been partying hard for a good while by then and stopped just in the nick of time, before I had some really serious problems to deal with. It's not that I was drinking so much I had to go to rehab or was losing jobs—but then again, I really don't know. I don't know what jobs I didn't get because of my lifestyle, or because I was a Playmate, for that matter. I'm sure there was stuff going on behind closed doors: "Should we see her?" "Nah, she's a Playmate, forget it." It may be that some people were looking at me thinking, *She was stoned during that audition.* All I knew was that the time had come. I stopped drinking and doing drugs, and I didn't miss it.

Gene and I did have some things to work out in the early days. He had a real problem with some of the ways I expressed myself, for example. I had picked up a few New York words and phrases from him, such as *scumbag*, which I loved and used everywhere. I also used the phrase *shut up* to mean "No, get out, I don't believe it." He did not care for that at all. I used it a few times and the last time, I guess, was one time too many. We were driving somewhere, and he pulled over and said, '*Shut up*' is not a phrase I ever want to be told or hear again from you." He was not kidding.

I was surprised. I said, "What, you mean '*shut up*'? It doesn't mean for you to literally close your mouth. It's a saying, for God's sake. Are you not from around here, or what? It's just an expression. You're in America now. It's not a sign of disrespect." This was the closest thing we've had to an argument to this day.

Generally it was small stuff we had to work out and get around in the beginning of our relationship. Gene spent so much time on the road touring, surrounded by people saying "yes" to his every request, that it was hard for him to come home to me. I was always a bit of a troublemaker, and was never afraid to talk back to him. He got yessed to death on the road, but he wasn't going to get it from me. He'd always had diva girlfriends, and I'm sure part of that personality type is attractive to him.

Gene was fascinated by the fact that I hadn't finished school, that I had been a "bad girl." I'm sure at the very beginning he was wondering to himself, "Why do I like her so much?" Bottom line: he has a double standard. There's a standard for girls on the road, and a standard for girlfriends. From the first night in the wine cellar at the Playboy Mansion, I was definitely "girlfriend" material, and he had high standards where I was concerned.

When Gene finished his tour he moved in with me—and Tracy and Ruben—and put his New York place up for sale. He was very concerned about the legal ramifications of actually living with me and wanted to be sure he didn't "owe" me anything. He was scrupulous about paying the rent, which, in the grand scheme of things, wasn't much money. I don't imagine it was cheap when Cher redecorated his New York apartment—though I had certainly enjoyed it when I was there. All things considered, I was a pretty inexpensive girlfriend.

So Gene moved in with us and learned to drive. It just wasn't realistic to live in Los Angeles and not know how to drive. This was a very big lifestyle change for him. He'd had a limo and driver when he'd spent time in L.A. before, though it had never been for extended periods of time. Gene bought Lionel Richie's secondhand Rolls-Royce and proceeded to run into everything in town. I suggested that he carry a large amount of cash in his pocket every time he went out driving so that he would be able to pay off everyone he hit on the spot. Truly, he was and is the worst driver I've ever seen. To this day, whenever possible, I try to take two cars to wherever we're going. To avoid conflict, I think it's best for

WHY WERE WE IN DISNEYLAND WITHOUT ANY CHILDREN?

couples to have separate cars and separate bathrooms.

We lived together very happily in the apartment with Tracy and Ruben for about six months or so. I must have been feeling pretty domestic, because I became a very enthusiastic baker. We had recently been on that New York dessert binge, and the craving for baked goods stayed with me. I asked my mom for some recipes, and Gene was crazy about my oatmeal-raisin-nut cookies. He couldn't get enough of them, so much so that he encouraged me to sell them. We actually considered starting a cookie business for a while, but then Mrs. Fields beat me to it, so it never really got off the ground. Plus, I didn't see that kind of business as my future; I was involved in all kinds of acting projects.

Life was a flurry of activity. Gene and I were both globe-hopping because of our work. There wasn't time to notice the little things most people criticize each other about after they've been together awhile. After the first few years they have time to obsess on how she really hates the way he does this, or how much her little habit bugs him. But we didn't.

Gene was preparing to go back out on the road and said to me one day, "I have to go back on tour; I think I'm going to buy a house here. Would you like to look for one while I'm gone?" I started checking into houses for him. When he got back we went to look at them together. There was one particular house we both liked; it was fully furnished because the owners were still living in it. It was a small ranch-style house, perfect for two people. But its big draw was the huge lot; it was a large property in Beverly Hills. We thought it would be a great investment. (It certainly turned out that way; it's where we still live today, though in a bigger house.)

Gene asked the couple, "How much cash will it take for you to walk away and leave all the furniture?" They came up with a price, he paid it, and they left with just their clothes. Gene and I moved in and even though there were a lot of things we wanted to change, we were so busy that we didn't do anything to it. We'd wake up in the mornings and just see each other briefly before taking off for work—auditioning or actually shooting a film or television role for me; rehearsing, handling his other business, or touring for Gene. We both loved the property, though, and now we had a little house that we called home base, where we could meet.

The first year we were dating, I used to go out with my friends

A LITTLE TAE KWAN DO TO GET IN SHAPE FOR A FILM.

and come home at midnight, and Gene never even asked, "Where were you?" He'd just be sitting at home, working, usually, and when I came through the door, he'd say, "Hey, come over and watch this with me!" He was always just happy to see me. It was so cool, and it made me want to never do anything to damage our relationship. This kind of behavior from both sides was unheard of in my love life. I'd been accused, followed, brow-beaten—and now I wasn't even being asked where I had been. Not that I'd been anywhere questionable.

Some girls might have seen Gene's attitude as an insult, as not caring, but he meant it in the best, most respectful way. He has taught me many things about tolerance and self-worth, but this was one of the biggest lessons I've learned from him. Gene's actions made me want to behave respectfully toward him. I thought, *I really like feeling this way. I want to behave well for us.* It felt good; it was easy. It's so much easier to let go of suspicion and speculation and making something of nothing when the person you're living with comes home.

One of the things that makes our relationship work so well was that we never did any of that stuff. You've got to leave the doghouse door open, because they'll come home eventually. Gene had been in (brief) monogamous relationships before, but he always had a wandering eye. I think he'd always thought, *Well, it's not going to last forever.* He always felt safe; free to walk away. He can't walk away now, of course, because of our children, but it's not bugging him, because he's not married. And I still don't ask him where he's been, with whom, or when he's coming home.

Sure, there were other guys who would have married me, but it doesn't count if they're not the one you want. I could have had six husbands by now. I don't have a "husband," but I have Gene.

CHAPTER NINE

She Works Hard for the Money

Everybody I worked with told me that I had an incredible ability to be "me" while speaking someone else's words—always a nice compliment for an actress. The word in the industry at that time—the straight-to-video market in the eighties—was that I was technically brilliant—a precious commodity, because there was a lot going on, and it was very fast-paced and budget-conscious. I knew how to set up my shot and what light to ask for, and could specify which filter I wanted; I picked up all of this knowledge by observing.

I did much of my own hairstyling, makeup, and wardrobe on these movies. I learned to take charge of my own look because, first of all, no one ever knew what to do with me, and second, the process was always very rushed. They'd just slap some makeup on me and send me out the door. They'd put black rings around my eyes and nothing else, or blush in the strangest places. This is one of the reasons I always showed up on time: I needed the extra time to redo whatever had been done to me. It was a quick education on how lighting and filters really worked. I got very proficient at getting myself camera-ready, leaving the crew to just powder my nose and fluff out my hair.

We used to put bright neon merkins on before filming, but only after writing something like "Fuck you" over it. Or a little sign you'd paste on yourself that said, "Camera, get out of my ass!" That way the director had to keep your full-frontal nudity out of the shot. If the note or merkin were filmed, the take would be ruined. I would negotiate it all out. I'd say, "Look, you can pan up and down to your heart's content while I fake away, but you cannot go there." First of all, full frontal nudity means another rating. And secondly, people take stills off videos and out of context, and post them on the Internet. Some of them really look bad. There are some stills of me floating around from scenes shot with, I thought, plenty of fog—but apparently not. Topless I had no problem with. What are boobs, after all? Who cares? Aside from a desire to look neither fat nor bad, I never had a problem with nudity, but maybe I should have. I certainly came from a very conservative background. Maybe too conservative, and that's why I was so willing to burst out of my shell. At some point I sure did!

Filming in the nude could be nerve-racking, though—particularly love scenes. While I was kissing the guy it was always in my mind that it had to look good, that he had to look really

AN IDEA I HAD IN THE
EIGHTIES FOR A COMIC
STRIP COME TO LIFE CALLED
DELTA TEAM. WE PITCHED
IT AROUND HOLLYWOOD,
BUT IT NEVER GOT MADE.

good, because I did not want to shoot the scene over and over again. I always wanted to do it right the first time, otherwise we could be there all day long. You'd be surprised at how many film virgins I had. I was always Mrs. Robinson with these young guys. Even when I was in my twenties I played older, because I looked and sounded older. I never had the young bimbo look or sound. I usually played someone who could haul off and kick some ass at the end. I started moving away from being arm candy—the reason men were running around with guns—to being the one who was running around with a gun. This was much more fun. There was a crossover time where I had to be sexy and half-naked and run around with guns, but it gradually evolved into me just kicking ass all the time.

I worked constantly in the straight-to-video market. I did at least 45 of these projects, but many of the titles escape me now. Often all that separated my kind of movies from the A movies was the budget. Some, of course, were just bad, but most had perfectly decent scripts. If Jack Nicholson had been starring they would have been great. But we didn't have the budget or Jack, so they weren't. We did the best we could with what we had. We were working in the genre that was a cut above a C movie, but not an A movie either. I was Queen of the B's.

When I did get a small part in a major movie, like the part I had in *Detroit Rock City* with Eddie Furlong, I was surprised at the difference between genres. That film had a budget ten times bigger than anything I'd ever been involved with. But can I tell you how boring it was, just to sit and wait? What I learned from doing a "bigger" movie was that it meant a lot more waiting. A lot more time wasted because they have the money and the time. When an actor didn't like his performance, the director gave him another take. Or if the director didn't like it, he'd say, "Let's do it again." They do take after take after take. I would be going out of my mind. "We have it. It's in the can. You can just *tell* people we did a hundred takes!" I was used to a much faster pace, like television. In fact, I preferred television, especially sit-coms.

I could, however, see myself getting spoiled by the budget and perks of a major film production. The food was better. The hotel rooms were better. The makeup and hair people were better. Just the general production values, of course, are what make movies "Movies." You know, syrup blood versus real special effects in the action movies. When deciding about doubles and the technical aspect, it revolves around the affordability of both the effects and the talent. So much of it's computerized now; it sure wasn't like that when I started.

In the straight-to-video market my stunts were mostly my own, and there was no budget for retouching or enhancement. Then there was what we in low-budgets call "scene stealing." I was doing a film once in Century City and we all jumped out of a van, shot the scene, and ran away before we were caught without the proper permits. We did the same thing downtown—the director and I rode in the van with the cameraman, who sneaked shots of me descending a big stairway in a famous downtown building, speaking my lines. I dubbed them in later.

In the eighties, straight-to-video was a perfectly good market. Andrew Stevens and I had a couple of the all-time best-selling

NICK ON THE SET WITH ANDREW STEVENS, PLAYING WITH FAKE BLOOD. IT RUNS IN THE FAMILY.

HOLLYWOOD HYPERLINK
WEB SITE DIRECTORY

SEARCHING THE STARS

The Web's premier movie database shows surprisingly eclectic interest in films and celebs.

As Hollywood players contemplate ever bigger forays onto the World Wide Web to take their (assumed) rightful place as new-media power-houses, they are colliding headfirst into the reality that Internet users often chart their own course. And while mindful of fancy film and TV marketing, the ultimate shape of the Internet — as shown by these recent top searches on the Internet Movie Database (www.imdb.com) — will be an unusual mix of current hits, obscure celebs and some genre favorites that will never die.

"Men in Black"

The Internet Movie Database has grown from a part-time hobby to the leading source for movie credits, reviews and other info. As of June, the IMDB sported some 1,642,728 filmography entries covering 448,214 actors and crew and 109,941 films. This phenomenal resource is fed by user input of information and corrections, received at a rate of between 50,000 and 75,000 per week, making it a comprehensive, self-correcting, bottom-up database.

Harrison Ford

Results for top title searches show a mix of recent hits ("Men in Black," "G.I. Jane," "Batman & Robin") with perennials ("Star Wars") and advance interest in sequels — some coming soon ("Scream: The Sequel") and others only assumed ("Men in Black II") but for which the IMDB — like the production charts in the trades — is already tracking information. "The Game," the first feature release by PolyGram, is also showing good traffic, a measure of the effectiveness of the traditional media campaign. As in recent months, the top actor searches are a mix of the usual suspects — Tom Cruise, Harrison Ford (still riding high almost two months after "Air Force One") and Mel Gibson) — Internet faves Teri Hatcher and Pamela Anderson (no indication whether those searches were driven by a desire for information or ribald pictures) and such direct-to-video stalwarts as Shannon Tweed and Tracy Scoggins (on surfers' minds presumably because of her recent replacement of Claudia Christian on the sci-fi TV show "Babylon 5."

— S. V. McKim

TOP TITLE SEARCHES		TOP ACTOR SEARCHES	
1.	"Men in Black"	1.	Harrison Ford
2.	"Scream"	2.	Shannon Tweed
3.	"Star Wars"	3.	Tracy Scoggins
4.	"Star Wars: The Special Edition"	4.	Pamela Anderson
5.	"Contact"	5.	Mel Gibson
6.	"The Game"	6.	Demi Moore
7.	"Men in Black II"	7.	Will Smith
8.	"G.I. Jane"	8.	Tom Cruise
9.	"Batman & Robin"	9.	Sandra Bullock
10.	"The Lost World: Jurassic Park"	10.	Robert De Niro
11.	"Scream: The Sequel"	11.	Sharon Stone
12.	"The Fifth Element"	12.	Quentin Tarantino
13.	"Braveheart"	13.	Teri Hatcher
14.	"Jerry Maguire"	14.	Nicolas Cage
15.	"Independence Day"	15.	Brad Pitt

Source: Internet Movie Database. Figures from Aug. 16-Sept. 14

straight-to-video movies; he did very well with those. I got producer credit on a couple of them, but most of them were buyouts, which means you are paid a certain lump sum for two or three weeks work; and that's it. No residuals. One year I did seven movies. They'd just shoot my part out and do the rest after I'd gone. If my salary was what cost the most, they'd shoot all my scenes in the first two weeks. Then I'd be wrapped and on to my next project while they finished up. I lost track of many of these films; some were retitled or I wasn't told when they were released.

If only I had been five foot seven, I would have won so many more parts! I was just too tall. I towered over Andrew Stevens and the other actors, but we did lots of projects together. Andrew just stood on stuff; he didn't care. He was a great guy that way. He hired me many times when he started producing and found scripts with me in mind. We had a lot of fun, but there were many famous actors I read for parts with who were intimidated by my height. Guys just didn't want to look smaller. Surprised?

There were many actors over the years I probably would have had big crushes on, had I not been so involved with Gene. Michael Pare, for example, was just a beautiful man. I had such a good time with actors on so many movies. Gene would joke around with me when I came home at night, "So, did you suck face today?" "Yes," I would mock-complain, "Andrew Stevens stuck his tongue down my throat again today." "That's my man," Gene would say approvingly. We were never jealous of each other's work life. He knew I was not being diverted emotionally. Gene is not a jealous guy; he's not insecure in that way.

Gene was never my career adviser. If he had been I probably would have made a lot more money and lasted longer in the business. I was working so steadily when I met him that he didn't presume to give me any advice, nor did I give him any advice about KISS. At the beginning, of course, we weren't sure where our relationship was going or how serious it was going to be. We were both very busy working on our respective careers.

The night I met him at the Playboy Mansion Gene had just wrapped his role as the villain in *Runaway*, his first foray into acting. He was cast in a couple of projects after that as an actor—a bad actor; that's part of his charm. Everything with Gene is so overdone when he acts. He puts on his newscaster voice and starts talking in a very deep, serious tone. I'd say, "What are you doing? You don't talk like that, why are you doing it now?" And he'd say, "Well the script calls for this." "Gene," I'd tell him, "they want *you*. Just be *you*. That's who they hired, that's who they want to see." I think he gets nervous and has a real mental block about remembering a lot of dialogue. Though after all these years of remembering lyrics and chords, vocals and stage directions, it seems he would be quite comfortable with acting.

I could always memorize pages and pages of dialogue. Which is funny, because I can never remember anyone's name. But dialogue—throw it at me. I can remember tons of it, especially when it's well-written and the conversation really flows. Gene says, "I don't know how you can remember all that. How do you do it; I can't ever remember what I'm supposed to say." When we watch television and see a show like *The West Wing* where they all talk so quickly and have such long, complicated conversations, he just marvels. I say, "Gene, stop worrying about how you're saying your lines. Stop thinking about you and think about what's going on. Then you'll get it." This is advice he doesn't understand. Everything in his life is about appearances; a large part of his job is overacting and theatrics. The subtleties escaped him.

There were so many times critics said, "She's just about to break out," or "She'll be the next big thing." You keep thinking, if you just get that one thing, that next role...And then—crickets—all of a sudden you're too old for that one big role. I was too tall, too pretty, too young, and then too old. There were so many near-misses with real fame, but I don't tell these stories with melancholy.

Warren Beatty called me in to read for a film role when he was involved with Madonna. I met him at a restaurant, and he asked me to go somewhere with him to talk about the project. "You know, I work very closely with my leading ladies," he told me. I'm sure he did, but I just headed home. I got a call a few days later from Warren at home. "How's Gene?" he asked. "Fine," I said, "How's Madonna?" And that was the end of that, until years later, when I saw him being interviewed at a restaurant while I was trying on sunglasses nearby. I walked over to where he was sitting and said, "Hey, Warren—this one, or that one?" showing him both pairs. He said, "That one." I later read the writer's description of what had happened in *Vanity Fair*: that a voluptuous blonde in thigh-high

BATHING SUIT PHOTOS – THEN AND NOW (24 YEARS' DIFFERENCE)

boots had approached him, asking whether or not she should buy these glasses. Warren told the writer that he didn't know who I was, that things like that happened to him all the time.

I guested on a lot of television shows—*Frasier, Married With Children, Wings*—all the big sitcoms. But still nothing happened; I never broke out in a big way. Odd things happened, too. On *Married With Children*, I played myself. I kept asking them, "Are you sure about this?" On another show they were going to use my name for my character, but I thought of a better name, a really trampy porn-star name, so they went with that. Sometimes the writers would see the humor about my level of fame, but I wasn't sure that my fame was quite as wide as they thought, and I wasn't sure anyone would get the joke. They would want to do a joke about the movie sequels *Night Eyes 3, 4, 5, 6* and *7*. I thought it was too obscure; that if they hadn't seen the first straight-to-video films, people wouldn't get it. But the *Night Eyes* sequels turned out to be very successful for their time.

It's all on a bigger scale now. Everything in the business has evolved. The quality of straight-to-video (or DVD) is better. The crap is crappier, big hits are bigger, and sex is sexier. Characters are humping and giving blow jobs every week on *Sex and the City*. That was absolutely unheard-of on television in the eighties. At that time, my simulated sex scenes in straight-to-video movies were

considered very trampy. When I see my old movies now, they're boring! But they were so risqué at the time—not porn, but very titillating. These movies had enough of a plotline so late-nighters wouldn't get too bored, and enough sex to keep them watching. I just tried to rise above the material and make it better. I knew that the "A" list writers wouldn't be writing material for me anytime soon, so I had to do the best I could with what I had.

I have a small fan base, so I always know when one of my projects is on television. A lot of times, though, people will come up to me and say, "Don't I know you from somewhere...I just can't place you." That's the kind of fame I've always had. They can't think of my name, or where they saw me, but they know my face. I've always been a little under the radar. It's been good, though; very good. I'm just glad to be working at all.

CHAPTER TEN

*N*icholas

I think in life it is better to be the one who is adored rather than the one who is doing the adoring. Everyone's mother says, "Make sure he loves you more than you love him," for a reason. It's a good rule of thumb, and it doesn't even necessarily have to be true, as long as you believe it. If you really believe that he loves you more than you love him, you're on the right track. And if he really believes that you love him more than he loves you, then you're both in a really good position. Both sides are happy when they have that feeling. And Gene and I both have that feeling...always have.

There is one area where I will not compromise in a relationship, and I know Gene wouldn't either, if he should ever get into another one. Which he won't—I'll make sure of that. That place is being completely honest, not playing games.

And he was honest. Gene had a spiel (that I've now proved to be at least half untrue). He always said very adamantly, "I do not want to have children, ever. It is not something I think I would be good at or wish to do. And I never, never want to get married."

The first two years Gene and I spent together were so great, so joyous and just so much fun. I had never been treated so well in my life by anyone. He said he was happy too. Of course the topic of marriage and children came up, but most guys say they don't want them. I took it with a grain of salt. There aren't too many men out there saying, "I can't wait to get married and have a child." Sometimes, of course, I'd ponder my situation. I'd think, *What, I'm going to spend 20 years with this guy and then wake up one day and be 50, and I won't be able to get another guy, and I still won't be married? It can't happen to me!* And here it is, 22 years later: I'm nearing 50, and I'm still not married, but it doesn't feel like it. And I mean that in a good way—a very good way.

After a couple years together Gene told me definitively that he wasn't going to marry me. As I said, that was nothing new; every guy I ever knew told me that, but I always thought marriage was a given. Like so many little girls, I was raised watching Disney movies in which the heroine marries the prince. My mom had a wonderful marriage until shit happened. All my friends, men and women both, were getting married, some for the second time. I loved Gene, and I knew he loved me. I just felt like, "Hey, wait, when do I get the party, the celebration, the wedding?" It's never been a deal breaker, though. I'm not laying down an ultimatum that I can't live up to. I'm not leaving if Gene doesn't propose, which puts me in a peculiar catch-22.

I couldn't change his views on the marriage issue. We were happy, we were in love, no one was going anywhere; but he was not getting married. So we decided to draw up legal papers that spelled out our living arrangement. I have to admit it was rather devastating at the time, but I was working my ass off, making lots of money, and soon enough I just had to say, "What do I care?" On the other hand, it was also kind of comforting, because he took the trouble to write it down, to make sure I was taken care of no matter what happened. He loved me more than I thought, more than I hoped. It proves once again that love and marriage are not the same thing.

The big issue with Gene and marriage, I believe, goes back to his father leaving his mother, and her not knowing what to do, and being poor. But you know what? His mother did fine, and so did mine. I don't know why he is so adamant about not getting married; it borders on "Methinks thou dost protest too much." My God, whenever anyone mentions the word marriage the man goes off on a rant. We all know how he feels; he wrote a whole book about it. But how long do I have to be called *my girlfriend, mother of my children, my lover?* Aren't all of these things the same as "my wife?"

I faced the fact there is not another guy on earth who wants to avoid marriage as much as Gene does, at least from a financial standpoint. Look, I think most men who could have everything exactly the same as it was in their lives—the sex, the companionship, and the children—without getting married, would probably choose not to marry. Gene was absolutely not going to budge. One person had to give up something in our situation, so I gave up my dream of finding a conventional Prince Charming and getting married. I learned that Prince Charming apparently has several different looks, and Gene learned I wasn't giving up on motherhood.

One thing I knew for sure was that I wanted to have children. I had known from our first few months together. I didn't know when or how it would happen, but I knew I had to change Gene's mind about having a family. Because Gene was "it." And if Gene was "it," then they were going to be his children. I had already compromised on the marriage part, but there was no way I was giving up on having children. At some point I knew we were going to have to discuss it.

As usual, Gene was the one doing all the discussing. He was the one saying loud and clear, over and over, "I don't want children. I don't want to be a father. I don't want...I don't want..." So I asked, "Well, what do you want? What do you want out of me, of this, of us?" And he told me, "I want what we have. Isn't it good like it is now?"

I reminded him, "You didn't even want that. You weren't looking for a relationship when we met. I don't think you know what you want. I'm going to *tell* you what it is you want!"

Around the five-year mark I felt a little restless, like "Somebody's got to make a move." We needed to clear all of this up. We'd had The Discussion at the two-year mark, when we signed the papers concerning our living arrangements, but I could still not quite wrap my mind around the idea that I wouldn't be able to change his mind about having a family. Until I could accept this idea, I had a little nagging feeling in the back of my mind: *I really love him, but, but, but...* The little tick-tock of my clock was starting. I knew I wanted children someday, and I was sad because I thought it might not be with Gene. I was giving the relationship my all, but it was never going to be enough for me without kids. I was happy and not happy. It was bittersweet.

Given all that, it was still a complete surprise when I discovered I was pregnant. Gene had returned home after being on the road for a long time, and we'd had a very passionate reunion on the bathroom floor, rug burns and all. I had a funny little feeling the next morning that something had changed. A fleeting thought went through my mind, but I pushed it away: *Nah, it can't be.* I certainly had not planned it physically. There would have come a time, as I got older, when I would have put my foot down about having children, but I wasn't at that point. I was on the pill, I was using contraceptive sponges, and so to say it was a shock when I confirmed that I was pregnant would be an understatement. What were the odds, I wondered, if you had sex every day for five years…?

I told my sister Tracy, who was very excited. My own feelings were more mixed. *Will he be angry? Will he think I'm trying to trap him?* I had two options. One, I could get rid of the baby and keep the guy, or keep the baby and the guy would leave…*maybe*. I decided I was keeping my baby. I had never known another man like Gene; every other guy I had ever been with was a drinker, a druggie, or just emotionally unavailable. I had never even wanted anyone else's children, and there were a few millionaires I could easily have tricked if that kind of behavior was in my makeup. It came down to this: I was 33 years old and I wasn't getting married anytime soon, but I was going to have this baby. I had already had one abortion. I started counting backwards. That baby would have been 15 years old. It didn't take much thinking before I decided I was not going to do that again. All these thoughts were running through my mind, and I just decided, "I'm keeping it. I'm working, I can manage if he doesn't want anything to do with it."

I held that thought firmly, and I got ready to break the news, but I just couldn't seem to find the right time. One evening we went to a big charity event at the Santa Monica racetrack. The news was burning a hole in my heart. We were standing around with Sherry Lansing, the head of Paramount Pictures; Joyce Bogart, whose charity event were attending; and several other people. I was so petrified, I couldn't understand a word of what anyone was saying; it was all just background noise. All of a sudden I blurted out, "I have something to tell you."

Gene was, and is, always great about giving me my own light. He would get out of the way when it was my turn for the spotlight or when someone wanted to interview me. If we were going down the line of paparazzi at a premiere and they asked me a question, he would stand out of the way or move entirely out of the picture frame. It was really sweet. So at this moment he was not noticing my panic. He got the usual expectant look on his face that said, "She's going to speak, and it will be wonderful." I felt sorry for him. I was going to drop a bomb on the man who had told me adamantly, so many times, that he would never have children or want them. I couldn't hold it in any longer. There was safety in numbers; we were surrounded, and by women. So I said, "You're going to be a dad."

The blood drained from Gene's face. I was glad we were in a public place. He couldn't throw a fit or start screaming or do anything crazy, but I had absolutely no idea what kind of response I would get. The people with us slipped away silently, and Gene took my arm and led me a few feet away.

"I'm pregnant," I clarified.

"Are you sure?" he said, when he could speak.

"Oh, I'm pretty sure," I told him.

"Well, what are we going do about this?" he asked me.

"Well, I'm having a baby. I don't know what you're going to do, but that's what I'm going to do." The words were tough but I was shaking. I figured this was it; this was the end. I was prepared to hear, "Well, good-bye, have a nice baby and a nice life." Although that kind of dumping would have been out of character for Gene, you never know how a cornered animal will react.

We drove home in the car together that night, and all he could say was, "Shannon. Shannon." Repeating my name, over and over. I was trying to make light of it, saying, "Gene, Daddy?" But he was just stunned into silence. For once. He had a helpless, throw-your-hands-in-the-air look on his face for days. For the first time in his life he had no control over a situation, and he was angry, surprised, worried, and helpless, though I thought I could perceive a tiny glimmer of excitement.

I have to say that all the signs pointed to us not making it. He had been so clear about not wanting a family; I was afraid that he wouldn't be able to get past the feelings of anger and betrayal. I really wanted to make him understand that this wasn't a con or a trap I had set to snag him. A few tense days later I laid it out in kind of a pathetic way. I told him, "I can live here and have the baby, or I can live by myself or with my sister and have the baby." What I didn't do was give Gene the option of not having a baby. It was A or B—I'll have the baby here, or I'll have the baby somewhere else, *but I'm having the baby.*

He remained stunned. He didn't like either choice; and he knew that suggesting I have an abortion would have been an extremely bad idea on his part. I wasn't giving up this baby. With the genes of the only straight and intelligent man I'd ever really loved? I think not!

Even though I didn't want him to feel in any way held captive by this, in essence he was trapped. He was going to have a child now, and although he would not have to deal with it physically if he didn't want to, he would have deal with it emotionally. I felt sorry for him as he struggled with a situation he had not bargained for, even if I knew he would make a great father.

I steeled myself for anything, but I knew I would be fine on my own. I was not going to terminate my pregnancy if he left me. Women raise children on their own all the time. My mom had raised hers, and I had friends who'd done the same. I wasn't particularly scared of the prospect; I was ready to be a mother. All

I could do was go ahead, just live my life day to day, and wait to see what Gene would decide. At the time I was doing a movie with Bill Maher, and it was very wacky being pregnant on the set. I was strengthened by talks with Adrienne Barbeau, who'd been trying to get pregnant for a long time (she has since had twins) and so had a very sympathetic ear. She was supportive and comforting, as were my sister and other close friends.

Gene didn't walk away. I had already planned to go visit him on KISS's European tour that year, and even though I was three months pregnant, I didn't change my plans. Gene was starting to warm up to the idea by the time he left for the tour, but there was still a hint of anger. He felt like he'd been had—the one thing he'd sworn over and over that he did not want. I sympathized, but not enough to give in.

I was happy with my decision, and even happier that he hadn't just taken off immediately. I grew bigger and bigger and decided to have the amniocentesis testing. I thought when the results revealed more about our baby, maybe Gene would feel differently about everything. I had joined him on tour and we were in London when I got the call from the doctor, who told me it was a boy. I was absolutely thrilled, jumping up and down on the bed, and Gene all of a sudden got very excited. From that moment on he introduced me as, "This is Shannon. She is going to be the mother of my son."

It was a 360-degree turn.

A son: a mini-me, a clone. What could be better for an

PREGNANT WITH NICK.

egomaniac? Oh yes, Gene was happy. When he said, "She's going to have my son," I would counter, "I'm going to have *my* son." But it was all good-natured; we were both thrilled. We were on the same page now and started thinking of names. I liked Noah.

"Noah is a pretty big name to live up to," Gene countered.

"No, *Simmons* is a big name to live up to; *Noah* would be fine. That's just a boat and a few animals!"

The story broke in the tabloids, and we happily shared the news with our family and friends. There was plenty of other stuff still going on in our lives. At this time Gene and I each had our own stalkers. I had one in Los Angeles who wanted to kill Gene, because he believed the baby was his own, and Gene had a fan in London who had a different reaction. She actually came to the door of our London hotel room. I don't know how she got past security, but she managed. (Never underestimate a stalker.) I happened to answer the door and when she saw me she actually ran away, but then she returned. I told Gene, "You answer it this time, and tell her to get out of here."

He went to the door to reason with her, and that's when she made her offer: "You know, I could kick her in the stomach right now for you." We had already called security, so they were on the floor by that time and took her away. That was another turning point. He became much more protective, realizing what a valuable and serious thing my pregnancy really was. The remaining months went smoothly, with me trying to reassure him. "What do we do?" "How do you raise a child, feed it, stop his crying?" Gene was full of worries. I told him that I was reading up on it but was sure the answers would come in time.

We settled on the name Nicholas Adam Tweed-Simmons. When I gave birth on January 22, 1989, that was it! He was thrilled, elated— happier than I had ever seen him. "He looked at me!" "He grabbed my finger!" I knew babies don't really see that well and they'll grab anything, so I just laughed. Gene was immediately, madly, forever in love with Nicholas, his son, his clone, and his love. His wife? Not to be, though he was moved enough to tell me, "I want to apologize. I didn't know what I wanted."

I pointed out, "There are other things you don't know you want, too! But we won't go there, because it doesn't really matter anymore." Of course he went off and drew up more papers about how Nicholas would get stuff, and I would get stuff, and so on. We had everything but the wedding. Pensions, health plans, houses, but no wedding. "My God, all I have to do is knock you off and we'd be all set. I should get rid of you right now!" I joked.

Having Nicholas barely slowed me down; I continued to work constantly. As a working mother I had to deal with what every

NICK AT 9 MONTHS AND OUR FRIEND MONIQUE.

NICK'S FIRST BIRTHDAY. WE OVERDID IT A LITTLE BIT WITH THE PETTING ZOO.

working mother does: finding reliable, trustworthy child care. I was torn, because I liked to do everything myself, but I also wanted to go back to work. I was busier than ever. I did have a lot of weight to lose, which wasn't hard. Exercising and breast-feeding took care of the 85 pounds I had gained during my pregnancy. (How had *that* happened?) It hadn't hurt the sex life either—the fatter I got during my pregnancy, the more fun Gene had with the junk in the trunk.

Very soon I was breast-feeding Nick in my trailer on the set of *1st and Ten*, starring O.J. Simpson, for HBO. I took Nick to Vancouver and all the way to Nice, France, for two months when I was shooting the television series *Fly By Night* for CBS. (My costar David James Elliot is now starring in his own show, *JAG*, and happily has children of his own.) I was lucky enough to find Nick's beautiful

A WARDROBE PHOTO FOR THE HBO SHOW
1ST AND 10 STARRING O.J. SIMPSON.

ON THE SET WITH MICHAEL DES BARRES,
WHO PLAYED MY HUSBAND ON A SHOW
FOR THE WB "MY GUIDE TO BECOMING
A ROCK STAR"

nanny Tawny, who came with us to these locations. She was an excellent nanny and a very nice girl, and I certainly give her a lot of credit for influencing Nick's manners and behavior in a very positive way. I could never thank her enough for doing such a tremendous job with Nick while I was working.

When Nicholas was two years old, we got a new live-in British nanny who was very proper and presentable. She was also a thief who stole a ring and a big wad of cash after she figured out how to open a wall safe in my bedroom. (It's always the smart ones you have to watch out for.)

Nicholas told me

one night, "A bad man came and shook a stick at me." I could not believe my ears; I was freaking out. "What bad man?" I asked him. "Nanny's friend, the bad man, he came in Mommy's bedroom," Nicholas told me. He wasn't hurt physically, but he reversed his potty training because the whole incident scared him so much. I was furious.

The nanny—let's just call her "Lisa,"—denied it up and down: She didn't know any guys; she didn't have a boyfriend; nobody had come in; Nicholas was making all this up. Then it occurred to me that I probably should go take a look in the safe. All the cash, a considerable amount, was gone. When people hear something like this, they say, "Well, just have her arrested." Believe me, I tried. She didn't have the money on her. It was long gone.

While I was hauling the stuff out of her room I found a picture of a man. I showed it to Nicholas and he immediately said, "Bad man!" I took it to the police, who told me that they could not do anything based on the testimony of a two-year-old. When Lisa came to work the next day I had arranged for someone to be right there to give her a lie detector test. Afterward, the expert who administered the test told me, "We're not even sure she is who she claims to be. She cannot answer a single question without lying." My sister and I threw all of her stuff in the driveway and told her to never come back.

Lisa had terrific references, but they all turned out to be bogus, because the girl who had been my nanny wasn't Lisa! She was using the name of another girl who had solid references. Boy, was that a new one. Why would anyone ever suspect that someone applying for a job was using someone else's name? You interview someone, have their references, call to check them, and you hear, "Oh, Lisa was great, dependable, she did a wonderful job." That's the usual way it goes. No one ever faxes you a photograph and says, "Tell me if that is Lisa." Now I do think that way.

BACKSTAGE WITH GENE AND A COVER BAND.

CHAPTER ELEVEN

Sophie

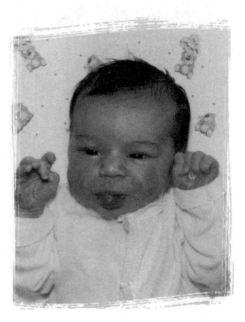

The second time I got pregnant, three years later, was not nearly as nerve-racking as the first. If I remember correctly, Sophie, another reunion baby, also was conceived on the bathroom floor,

SOPHIE – AGE ONE DAY.

this time so Gene and I wouldn't wake up Nick. Again, I called my sister Tracy first, and we talked about the best approach for telling Gene. In the end I just said, "Guess what, hon—surprise, again!" His response was, "Oh my God. Oh my God." I added, "Maybe this time we'll have a little girl!" "Oh my God. Oh my God," was all he could say to that.

Gene didn't seem to be any less frightened the second time around. On July 7, 1992, he once again anxiously waited for his child's birth at Cedars-Sinai Medical Center in L.A., holding my hand, cutting the cord and once again shedding tears of joy and pride. He didn't have to wait long; Sophie arrived much faster than Nick. Could Daddy be happier?! Or more frightened—a girl!

ME AND SOPHIE.

Sophie was a beautiful baby, born with a little birthmark on her cheek. As she grew up we told her that she was kissed by an angel or hit by a falling star. I would kiss the little chocolate mark on her cheek and make a wish. We told her she could have it removed whenever she wanted. She has said she wants to keep it, that it makes her special. (However, as I am writing this, Sophie is a beautiful 13-year-old young lady as who recently asked if it would hurt to have the birthmark removed. We'll wait for her final decision.)

Of course, that's not what makes Sophie special to us. Named after Gene's favorite actress Sophia Loren and my favorite film, "Sophie's Choice," she has as pure a heart as you could ever find. Sophie is a nurturing, mother earth-type child who shows great empathy and sympathy for all living things. She enjoys life to the fullest. She loves horses and dogs, laughing, and her girlfriends. She loves doing girlie things with me and adores her daddy—history repeating itself. Whatever she asks for is hers. Luckily, neither child abuses our generosity, because he's emptying his pockets every time he looks at them.

Gene proved to be a wonderful father to both son and daughter in many ways. After Sophie was born I continued to be very active, appearing in all kinds of films and television shows. (I had another 80 pounds to lose, but Billy Blanks' Tae Bo took care of that.) Gene made sure that I had lots of help with the children so I could juggle everything. He was a great help, himself. One day I decided the time had come for him to change a diaper. I waited for just the right moment. When Gene took off the diaper, Nicholas peed straight up into Gene's shirt pocket. I was hovering behind him, cracking up.

Sophie was a dream baby. Happy and independent, sweet and wise. Gene was so worried about how he would talk to a daughter. "I don't know what to say to a little girl. What if I break her, or drop her or hurt her feelings…?" It went on and on. Needless to say he fell madly in love with his little bundle of energy. He admires her spunk and bravery. Sophie will be the first one with her hand up and the leader of the pack, the first to cliff-dive and the one who loves easily. We fear as much for a broken heart as broken bones.

When the kids were babies Gene would feed them or bring them to me in the wee hours of the morning to be breast-fed. He rarely

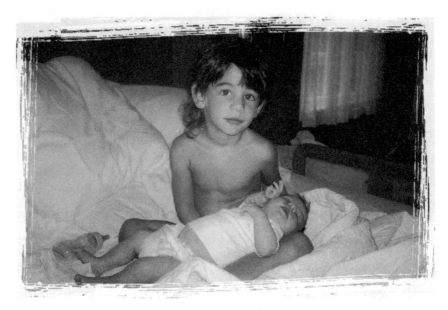

NICK AND SOPHIE.

slept through the night. He would wake up, check on the kids, and run to them when he heard crying or knew they were having bad dreams. Nick and Sophie mean everything to Gene. I remember admiring his protective instincts when the big earthquake hit L.A. Our house was shaking and I had barely opened my eyes from a deep sleep when Gene had already gathered the children and was standing with them in the doorjamb calling my name.

Gene was doting, loving and reliable, but he was also working and frequently on the road, so we traveled to see him, he traveled to see us, making sure the kids knew him and saw him as much as possible. When we were all together, we had wonderful times. From Chuck E. Cheese to McDonald's and Disneyland, we did all the things other families with young children did.

As parents, the one area of difficulty we had was discipline. I had been spanked a couple of times in my childhood, and Gene and I struggled over whether or not to physically discipline our children. We agreed that it wasn't for us or for them: we felt bad, they felt worse, and we just couldn't do it more than once. That doesn't mean it didn't work—it worked like a charm—but we figured there had to be a better way to teach good behavior than to hit a little body. We take a firm stand on rules in our home, and—knock on wood—our kids listen and have never done anything after their first spanking to warrant another. No always means no, never maybe,

MOM, BABY SOPHIE AND NICK.

and Gene and I make it a point to agree on things so the kids can't pit one parent against the other. They never have to be told to go to bed, get up for school, or do their homework more than once. Gene and I keep a united front. Kids need rules, and they're happier when they know what's expected of them and how they're doing. Praise is good.

I hope I can use some of what I've learned from my relationships to help my children as they grow up. My daughter will be horrified by some of the admissions in this book, but I want her to learn from my experiences. The things that I did as a teen go on with some of her friends too. I want to help Sophie make healthy choices in her love life. Hopefully she won't be looking for love in all the wrong places like her mother. I want her to understand that sex is fun when the time is right, but not a bartering tool. I also want her to learn from my mistakes, and more importantly, know that when you make a mistake, and we all do, it's never too late to change for the better. We are, after all, what we do now and who we are today.

I want to teach Nick about what girls really want, and how to have a healthy attitude about sex while understanding that no means no. Respect has become one of the most important aspects of a relationship to me, and I want both of them to respect the opposite sex and value real love. My kids might think it's a pain in the ass to have a parent who knows too much, but I find the good and usefulness in it. Gene might be oblivious to certain behaviors of teenagers, but I'm not. I am keenly aware, and plan to stay that way.

Since Nick and Sophie were born Gene and I haven't discussed marriage (other than a few wisecracks) or any of the other stuff that used to seem a lot more important. After you have kids you get your priorities straight in a hurry. They are what are important to both of us. Children, health, love, work—in that order for me—and even work has a whole new meaning.

QUIET ON THE SET.

SOPHIE TOOK OVER FOR A LITTLE ACTRESS WHO GOT TIRED DURING A MOVIE SHOOT, BUT SHE HASN'T ACTED SINCE. SHE WAS SUPPOSED TO PLAY SAD. THE DAY BEFORE I'D ACTUALLY HAD MY NOSE BROKEN IN A FIGHT SCENE GONE WRONG.

$\mathscr{G}$roupies

Sometimes women who don't know Gene and me personally will say to me, "Doesn't it bother you that he's out screwing around all the time?" If I say he's not, I look kind of foolish, like I'm in deep denial or something; if I say, "No, it doesn't bother me," I just look like an idiot. But the truth is: if I don't know about it, then it doesn't bother me. No one truly knows what goes on except Gene. What I do know is more married people cheat on their significant other than do partners who aren't married. I know he flirts; he flirts plenty. I see the "suave bolo" thing in his eye. He wants to make the girls swoon, and that's fine with me. After all, who wants a guy no one else wants? But he has never lied to me, and I don't think he cheats. I haven't heard any stories of infidelity, or at least no women have come forward, so speculating is all anyone can do. I choose to believe the best and believe him to be true to me, to our kids, and to our life together. Plus, I don't ever want to be petty or trivial with what we have, because it's worth so much to me.

When you're the girlfriend of somebody famous, rich or attractive, there will always be girls around trying to take your

PUBLICITY SHOTS FROM THE TOM SHOW.

boyfriend. With KISS there have always been aggressive groupies. It's amazing how many of them are out there; they're a hazard. There have been times when I've physically put myself in front of a girl who was just getting a little too hot for Gene in front of me or the kids. But come on, I can't be there all the time. Gene handles everything just fine when I'm not around. That being said, there are moments when I feel a certain disrespect, and it bothers me immensely when ex-girlfriends continue to call, visit, hint, flirt, write notes, or all of the above. It's been more than twenty years, ladies—he's not coming back!

I personally never did that groupie thing so I don't really understand it. With the exception of Tom Jones, I've never been a very good fan. I was always able to make the distinction between sexual cheating and emotional cheating. In my heart I don't really consider it cheating if you get, say, a blow job from someone whose name you don't know. I kind of think like a man in that regard. I'm not saying that it would please me by any means if my partner did that. Someone would have to pay, but I'm pretty sure I wouldn't end my relationship over it. I would be upset, but not "Fatal Attraction" upset.

Maybe I have this attitude because sometimes in the past I was the one for whom it was just sexual. Or maybe it's because I've seen all the groupies in action, and they really do move from one musician to another. Usually, they don't want to take your guy and marry him and live with him and have children with him and be emotionally involved. What they want is the excitement of being at the show and nabbing the dick onstage. That's thrilling. The whole idea is probably not that glamorous the next morning. It's a notch in everyone's belt, and then time to move onto the next one. What surprises me is that Gene does not appear to have more children!

As far as Gene is concerned, I know he hasn't fallen in love with anyone else since we met, and that's what's important. In my situation, part of the key to keeping a man in Gene's position happy is not to keep the reins loose, but to have no reins at all. Reins and cages are for horses and birds. Through the years, when Gene has called me, I've never asked, "Where are you?" Sometimes I don't even know what city he's in; but I know he calls me every day.

I didn't consciously decide to live my life this way; my behavior is a natural evolution of my respect for him. From the start, I never had any jealous or possessive feelings about him or our relationship. I'd had the boyfriends with whom I felt insecure and done that whole stupid, whiny "Why are you talking to her? If you want her, why don't you just go get her?" All those childish games—I just couldn't do anything like that to Gene. When my emotions and hormones do get the better of me, I'll try to get reassurance from Gene and tell him what I am feeling.

When I met Gene I wasn't policing him or keeping a sharp eye out in case he did something. I've learned if they're going to do something, they're going to do it. There is nothing you can say or do to stop a man from cheating if he's the cheating kind. If you're married and you quit giving your partner a sex life and an emotional life and support, you might force him to leave, but I don't know of any way to force a man to do the opposite—to love you and be faithful to you—if he doesn't want to.

Jealousy is pretty nonexistent with us. I don't dwell on it. I don't like feeling it, and I choose not to. It's a useless waste of energy, one of those feelings that sucks out all the good stuff from inside of you. When you're jealous and worried and nitpicking, it drains all the joy out of everything. It's natural, it's tempting, everyone's felt it, but you shouldn't indulge it, because it can wreak havoc on an otherwise normal, healthy relationship.

WITH GENE AT HIS
BIRTHDAY PARTY AT THE
SPORTSCENTER BOWL.

Gene and I have always had a calm partnership. Like the one my parents had before the accident, we don't fight (although I've had my crabby moments), and we have a healthy, playful sex life. In 22 years we may have agreed to disagree on many things, but we haven't had a fight. Gene said once, early on, "Let's never fight about the little things. If I leave my socks and shoes in the middle of the floor and you don't like it, I'll hire someone to pick them up." He was right; when you pick and pick about little things, you're probably unhappy in the relationship for other reasons. Instead, you need to pinpoint what's bugging you, work it out, and let it go. Yes, every relationship has compromises. That's very grown-up, compromising.

Gene and I have always told the truth to one another. I've always been very clear about what I want, which has never been

167

exactly what he wants. But I haven't loved him less just because he doesn't think the same way I do. I like the way he thinks, he likes the way I think, and we like each other just as we are. We had to figure out a way to work around our differences, because to me, Gene was the big prize. Not because he is a celebrity, because I've been there, but because he is sober, smart, and he loves me. He was and is an honorable man with a kind heart and, oh yeah, like I said, he loves me. That's big.

He's really great in the sack, too. Remember the candles, the bath, and the food at our first encounter in New York? That was nice—great, in fact—but I don't need it, which is good, as I've never seen it since. What I do need is attention when I need it, and Gene knows how to give it. He is, without a doubt, all man, all the time. The kind of man who's brave and shy, conceited and humble, manly and barely in touch with his feminine side. Well, there is no feminine side, but there is a soft side. He's adventuresome and traditional and predictable in a spontaneous way. He can find ways to surprise me in bed that I least expect, yet I expect it from him. I expect that I will always be pleasantly surprised by the way he touches me; handles me; and always, always makes sure I'm happy before he is. This unselfishness warms my heart and everything else.

At almost six feet tall I feel small and feminine when I'm with Gene, and while he clearly replaced a lot of my lost love from my father, he is in no way paternal to me. He's a slut, and I like it that way. He's a cheap and easy lay, ready at the snap of my fingers. He's proud of that, and that's okay with me. He can throw me around and leave me limp. Let's face it, it's good to play dirty. I will let you in on a little secret—that tongue! It's my second-best friend, and folks, it's not the size—but the speed that counts. Five speeds! He loves the fact that I feel weak-kneed in the bedroom, and he feels that's the one place he can get me to shut up!

I was well aware of what was available to me in terms of men at the time I met Gene. I had been out and about in L.A. It was pretty slim pickings from the pool I was swimming in, and I learned that it's very rare when a relationship comes along in which your feelings are reciprocated. One or the other is working too hard, trying to feel it; faking it; or settling. Gene and I did none of those things. I didn't feel like he was the last man I was ever going to meet. I liked him; I liked everything about him. His looks grew on me. I didn't look at him that first night at the party and fall over saying, "Wow." But as we grew closer what he was became very attractive to me. I appreciated him—his honesty, his loyalty, his initiative, and even his flaws.

So that's why I don't get petty with Gene, ever, because it isn't worth it. If he flirts with another woman, groupie or not, it doesn't mean anything. He's a man, why wouldn't he look at a beautiful woman? What do I want, a eunuch? I'll look at a handsome man, and Gene doesn't bug me about it, because it's just a fantasy. I have the hots for Tom Jones, to put it mildly. I love him, I want to eat him up. But I wouldn't ever really do anything if I had the chance, because then this wonderful feeling I have for him would be gone. Nothing could live up to what's in my head. In my mind Tom Jones would just look at me and I'd have an orgasm. And you know in reality he'd have to work at it, like very other guy. Nope, not going there; not going to spoil it.

My obsession with Tom goes way back to my childhood when we used to watch him on television. When I was 18 and working as a waitress at the Four Seasons Hotel in Ottawa, he played there once. I watched him and I wondered, could there be anything sexier than that? I was taking a break in the café when he came in for breakfast with his bodyguards. I almost fainted dead away. As he walked out I couldn't even glance in his direction. He was going past my table and I looked down at the floor, because if I raised my eyes any higher his crotch would be right there in my face. I was at eye level with Tom Jones's crotch—the stuff of my dreams. (Well, not really—I dream about his mouth.) I kept my eyes on his boots, which, coincidentally, were the exact same kind of boots Gene was wearing the night I met him, and still wears to this day: pimp boots, I call them.

I was staring at Tom Jones's high-heeled boots, thinking, *Oh my God. Oh my God. Please don't say anything to me because I'll die.* He stopped at my table; I was sitting there, wearing my little tiny black cocktail dress, getting ready to go back to work. I don't remember what the guard's name was, but Tom looked over and said something like "Hey Joe, she's a pretty one, isn't she?" And still I could not even look at him! The guy was like, "Yeah, yeah, come on boss, we've gotta go." I finally raised my eyes and saw a big belt buckle, and was overcome. *Oh my God, look down, look quickly down.* I will never forget it.

Cut to five or six years ago. Tom Jones was playing at the House of Blues. I said to Tracy, "We have to get in, because I have to see Tom Jones!" We got backstage passes from Ted Field, who is the father of my sister's children and the founder of Interscope Records, Tom's label at the time. Tracy was happy to come along and share my experience. She doesn't carry the same torch for Tom, but she knows how brightly mine burns. She remembers how, when we were kids, I used to watch him on television, and knew the words to every single song—wait—just like a groupie! I've never had this kind of reaction to anyone else. I don't care about any other celebrity, musician, anything—but Tom Jones just does it for me.

There Tracy and I were, sitting on top of a bar at the House of Blues, doing every hand movement and singing every word louder than his backup girls, who couldn't have been very happy with us. (Sober we were doing this; imagine how dangerous I was drunk.) We were really being obnoxious. After the show we went backstage and I said, "Tom, I have to meet you. My name is Shannon Tweed." He said, "I know who you are." I said, "You do?" I was completely shocked. "Well yes," he said, "you're Shannon Tweed." I snapped back to and said, "Oh yes, of course I am." I said, "I've got to tell you this story. When I was 18, I was working in this cocktail lounge…" I told him all about the belt buckle and how I couldn't bring myself to look at his face. I finished up by saying, "So I really have to lay one on you now. Do you mind?" He said, "I would love that." So I rammed my tongue in his mouth. Kissed the hell out of him. It was great. Great!

My sister piped up, "Hey, I want one, too." So she kissed him, too, and the second she was finished her boyfriend walked in. Ted was mortified that we were acting like such fools. We posed for pictures and said, "Let's give him a Tweed sandwich." We squished Tom in between us and took a bunch of shots. We were laughing, talking—having such a good time. Then he was pulled away by

MY SISTER TRACY AND I ARE SO ALIKE. WE HAVE THE SAME TASTE IN PHOTOGRAPHY, CLOTHES, MAKEUP, HAIR AND – SOMETIMES – MEN.

everyone coming backstage to congratulate him on the show, and I said to Tracy, "We have to go right now, because I don't want to see any more or know any more about him. This is perfect!" I still had my fantasy, I still loved him, and it was great. Great!

We went to Vegas last year and caught his show again, though we didn't go backstage. He saw us and waved to me, and that was so hot. So, as I've discovered with Tom Jones, I do know the feeling of being a groupie. I don't want to take him away from his wife or have a lifelong affair with him. I just want to do him, that's all, but I don't *really* want to do it, because then the fantasy would be gone. It's a weird thing. Tom, if you're reading this, I still want to do you, baby. Always have, always will. Every time I hear that line "It's not unusual to be loved by anyone" I just go crazy in the head.

Gene knows very well how I feel about Tom. I called him after that night at the House of Blues and said, "I just want to tell you that I totally tongued Tom Jones right in front of all the paparazzi, and I'd do it again in a second." He said, "That's okay, because I would do Sophia Loren in front of her two children if I could." "I know," I told him. "And I'd let you." He has always loved Sophia Loren. Remember, that's why our daughter's name is Sophie. I couldn't name my son Tom though; it would have taken the zing out of my mental affair with Mr. Jones.

Cut to Gene: He's on an airplane going to New York one day, and who's sitting next to him? Tom Jones. So funny.

I've only ever asked once for an autograph for myself. One night years ago, Tracy, some friends, and I were at Spago celebrating my birthday, and I approached Sean Connery. We were both standing in a long line for the loo. I said, "Hello Mr. Connery, I've always loved your movies and I would really appreciate an autograph if you have time." He blew me right off. He said something like, "I am here with my family having dinner if you don't mind," very coldly, in that Scottish accent. Tracy, who was with me, remembers this incident differently— she recalls him telling us to "Fuck off." Whatever words were used, he certainly wasn't gracious, and I felt really stupid.

I've been on the other side of that, and I sign the autograph no matter what. I remember once Suzanne Pleshette came up to me and said, "You know, I really like you. You're a good actress, I

NICK GETTING TALLER! A GOOD-LOOKING BOY.

TRACY, MOM, TRACY'S DAUGHTER EMILY, SOPHIE, ME, AND GRANDMA
FLORENCE (GENE'S MOM).

hope you get some better roles." I really liked her; I appreciated
her saying that to me. It was very nice. So it hurt that night when
Sean Connery was so dismissive. I've never asked anyone for an
autograph since then. It was just so devastating and embarrassing.
He was so rude, and I wasn't some schmuck off the street; I was
in the same restaurant having my birthday dinner! But Tom Jones
more than made up for it.

CHAPTER THIRTEEN

Ripoffs and Piss-Offs

Money. It's important. I always had big plans for what I would do with all the money I earned, but somehow I just kept spending it. This is where Gene and I really differ. Gene is all about getting money, saving it, not spending it, and being buried with it. He has enough money for three lifetimes, and he still panics if a week goes by when he's not bringing home the bacon. I just say, "Relax, take a break, enjoy life...," but that is how he enjoys life. He takes no joy in spending.

That's not to say that Gene doesn't spend plenty on the kids and me. He never skimps on us. And he's been really great about spending on our house, because left to his own devices, he'd be living in his old apartment in New York. The whole concept of spending money to create a really beautiful home was another element, like children, he didn't know how much he wanted in his life. But believe me, he wouldn't be doing it if he didn't enjoy it, because there is nothing I can make him do that he doesn't want to do.

It wasn't a big risk to build the house, just a big commitment. I'm constantly reassuring him: "It'll be okay, let's get some stones for the driveway, some new plants…" I have to poke and prod him every step of the way to put a waterslide in the pool or to upgrade anything. I really care about quality, whereas he thinks a door is a door is a door. He sees nothing inferior about a fiberboard door when compared with a beautiful custom-made door. He really, truly can stare at both doors all day and not see the difference. This is the man who said a room at Motel 6 is just as good as anywhere else. That's because he doesn't use anything except the toilet and the television and then he falls asleep. He's not the kind of man to sit around and appreciate the décor. To me, it's all about enjoying my environment. I like a room to make me feel warm, comfortable, and relaxed.

The only thing that's "him" in our home is the entrance. Gene did express a desire for a grand entrance hall—with a dome—for our new house, but that was only for the resale value. When we were designing the new house with architect Tim MacNamara, Gene looked at the plans and said, "Let's do a dome." I thought he was crazy. "What the *$(%* do you need a *dome* for?" He said, "Oh, come on, it'll look good, and it might down the line, later, you know…" I said, "What, for resale? Look, I'm not leaving. You can build your dome, and you can think it will add to the resale value, but I'm not leaving this house. Ever."

I didn't want the living room, dining room, or grand entrance. What I wanted, actually, was a new, not necessarily bigger, but

NEW house where the fuses didn't blow out every time I plugged in the blow-dryer, like it did in our original house. And I figured we didn't really need all that extra square footage; all we needed were rooms we would really use. Gene kept saying, "Yes, but the architect says, for the resale value..." I said, "Fine, then, I'm going to design all the stuff we'll really use: the kitchen, the family room, the bedrooms, the offices, and *my* bathroom. Separate from his, finally.

In the old house we were supposed to share a bathroom, but Gene didn't get to use it much because of his bathroom habits. He refuses to lock the door, and then gets mad when we walk in on him. He's always just reading a magazine on the toilet. I say, "Get out of there! What are you reading in there for?" I've never understood that. Well, maybe he feels it's the only place he can go

TRACY VERY PREGNANT WITH HER TWIN BOYS WITH MOM AND ME IN 2003.

and we won't follow him in—but he's wrong. If I could give only one piece of advice to couples it would be "Don't share a bathroom," meaning, don't use the bathroom at the same time. And close the damn door!

Gene's office on the other side of the house holds KISS gold and platinum records and every piece of KISS merchandise imaginable: posters, dolls, clothing, keychains—even pinball machines and coffins. It's great, fun stuff, and I appreciate it, but I said, "Look, I know this stuff has gotten you where you are today, but really, I don't want to look at it all the time. I'm not throwing up my centerfolds all over the walls, so don't you either. Let's separate our everyday life from our work life."

It's a tremendous amount of work to build and furnish the house, because Gene will not get involved (except for the dome). He pays for it, then walks away. When I need more money, though, he'll ask why, but then he doesn't want to hear the explanation. He doesn't want to hear where I'm going to buy it, where I'm going to put it, or why we should have it, but he does want to know exactly why I want more money. It's a challenge.

👄   👄   👄

Having other people in your house is always a challenge. We've experienced it in a couple of different ways, one resulting in a lawsuit, the other in a robbery (remember "Lisa"). We moved out of the ranch style house to a rental while we were building our new home. The rental was a tiny house, even smaller than the original. I wasn't working as much as I used to, so I decided to let one of the housekeepers go.

After our children were born, I had been busier than ever with work, and we usually had two housekeepers. If I went on location, I could take one, as a nanny, with me and the kids. The other housekeeper would stay with Gene in the house. The two used to rotate. I never wanted to be in the position of hiring someone new at the last minute to baby-sit my kids (or my man) if I suddenly got a job. The most important thing to me was that the kids were comfortable and familiar with their caretakers if Gene and I both had to work away from home at the same time.

By the time we were living in the rental, the movie roles were had slowly petered out, and I was only making sporadic television appearances. It looked like I wasn't going to be working on anything in the near future. If something came up, the kids would stay home this time, because they were settled in school and were old enough to know that I would be coming back. I just couldn't justify employing two housekeepers. One of them had a small child at the time, and the other was single with no dependents, so she's the one I let go. This woman turned around and sued us for racism, mental cruelty, sexual advances from me and Gene—anything and everything—you name it. I had supposedly yelled at her and beaten her down daily.

My first reaction was, "Oh, and you lived with this for how long? Five years you stayed with us when you're getting beaten down and humiliated every day? I don't think so!" She had found one of those ambulance-chasing lawyers who specialize in representing nannies who sue their celebrity employers. He approached our lawyers with the offer: "She'll take $125,000 to go away, and of course that way it won't make the papers."

I didn't give a damn if it made the papers. "Print anything you want, go right ahead, you are not getting a dime," was my attitude. I remembered the other nanny, "Lisa;" no one else was going to steal from me with my knowledge! The housekeeper lost a really easy job where she had been very well paid while working in a pleasant atmosphere. She was pissed because she would have to find another job, and suing was her way of making us pay. The battle was on.

Her lawyer went through our lives with a fine-tooth comb. Everything we ever said or did to each other over the past five years was up for examination. And it was all so boring and ordinary that her lawyer got very frustrated. It makes a difference in a lawsuit if you employ a certain number of people, because that way you'll be sued as a company or corporation. They were trying to show that we had lots of employees, so her lawyer was asking me questions like, "So how many people did you have on staff at all times?" I answered, "One."

"Come on now. What about your chef?"

"Chef? No. I do the cooking."

"Your driver?"

"You're looking at the driver."

"Your shopper?"

"You're looking at her!"

He truly couldn't believe how we lived. It was too ordinary, everyday—something had to be going on under the surface. And he dug for it.

Was I sure that Gene hadn't made a pass at her? I was quite sure. Why was I so angry, yelling at her all the time? I had never raised my voice to her in my life. She lost a good job; she was angry and upset about it; that was it. Our former housekeeper, the plaintiff, would show up in the deposition room, crying and saying, "Look at her! The way she's looking at me, that was how she looked at me every day! It made me sick, it made me cry!" It was so over-the-top. I was just sitting there looking at her very calmly. I could not believe how far she was taking it.

They went over the most ridiculous stuff with us. Had I fired her because money was tight? What about the diamonds Gene bought you this time and that time? I answered, "That had nothing to do with this. He's not going to buy her diamonds, too! One had nothing to do with the other!"

Then they played the race card, which was a joke. We'd dated, between us, a representative of at least seven other countries. You've got the wrong family on that one. Nor was it about her being an immigrant. Gene wasn't born in the U.S.; neither was I. Where you come from has nothing to do with anything. Neither one of us cares where you're from as long as you're honest and honorable and doing your job correctly.

They jumped on that. "So she was doing her job wrong?"

"I didn't have any work for her. That's all. I am not obligated to keep somebody on when there's no work for her to do. It is not my responsibility to take care of her financially for the rest of her life because she worked for me a few years. I am not her husband; I am not responsible for keeping her in the manner to which she became accustomed. I gave her three weeks' notice with pay." That hadn't been enough, obviously.

The legal proceedings made its way into the papers, of course. We made the *National Enquirer*: "Gene Simmons and Shannon Tweed's Nanny Sues for Racism, Sexual Harassment, Mental Cruelty." The subhead was something like: "Miss Tweed Repeatedly Berated Her." Blah, blah, blah.

They tried everything to get us to pay her off, but we would not budge. I was in litigation and depositions for a year over this matter. I said, "You know what? I have all the time in the world. You are not getting a thing. I'd rather have my lawyer buy new golf clubs than give you one red cent."

After a year of this we were just about to go to a jury trial and her lawyer made an offer: "Okay, we'll take thirty thousand dollars."

"No, no and no," was our answer.

"Okay, ten thousand."

"No. Not ten. Not a hundred. Not one dollar. You get nothing!"

Then the lawyer came to us directly. "I'm having second thoughts about the validity of my client's accusations." I said, "Oh,

NOT LOOKING BAD IN MY FORTIES.

now you're having second thoughts, because you're not getting any money? Still no! You're going to have to eat it. Whatever time you've put in, that's tough. Believe me, she's never going to pay you anything, and we're not going to pay you anything. Go away. We're going to trial."

Now here's an injustice in our justice system: they dropped the case. That was it, it was over. All the money we put out; all the time it consumed. People can just say whatever they please, and you have to prove you didn't do it! You are not innocent until proven guilty; you're presumed guilty until you prove that you're innocent. It was horrible; we had to defend ourselves against someone who was flat-out lying, trying to make a quick buck. There was no point even in countersuing her.

When it was all said and done, what we paid our lawyer was about the same amount the housekeeper had been seeking. But there was no other choice. Pay her or pay our lawyer—and we much preferred to pay him. What kind of precedent would we be setting by paying her? Gene was with me on this one; his principles wouldn't allow it either.

Now I'm not afraid to fire anybody. They know that we'll go all the way to the jury with them. We will not pay someone off; it's not going to happen. We do not negotiate with terrorists!

⬥ ⬥ ⬥

The second challenge we faced because of having people working in our house involved the theft of some jewelry that was very precious to me because of what it represented. But the story starts out with our theme of being honest, loving each other enough to compromise, and the special feeling we have as a family.

Christmases are interesting at our house. I like them traditional, and Gene doesn't like them at all. We light a menorah and have a tree because Christmas has never meant religion to me. I see it as a day of thanksgiving and joy for children. My kids are hard to please at Christmas, because they never want anything. I try to dream up things to surprise them, and they're always glad I did.

Poor Gene, he always gets clothes, because he doesn't like

toys or gadgets or cars. He writes everything down in a notebook, so no Palm Pilot for him. He has his old cell phone from years ago—"It's fine," he says, "it's working,"—while I have the latest camera phone with every accessory. He doesn't wear jewelry and doesn't care about his clothes (he'd wear the same shirt every day if I let him), so Christmas and his birthday are the times I buy him clothes—with his own money lately, poor guy.

The kids make him homemade presents, which of course he likes. Nick will get creative with his artful Christmas cards, always with a lovely note to us both. Over the years Sophie has made many handmade ceramic dishes to put change in. Each one has a personal inscription, so Gene loves them all. He is happy when I make him his favorite rice pudding or bring his favorite marzipan cake as a present. He's low maintenance that way, but high maintenance enough to keep me on my toes in other ways. He's like his mother. He likes things a certain way—not many things, but he wants what he wants the way he wants it. Toilet paper must be folded just so; coffee must be too hot and served in a paper cup so he can drop an ice cube in it; air conditioning must never blow in his face. Dogs must not be heard drinking; and birds are to be admired but not heard chirping. For someone who plays in a high-decibel rock band, it's eerily quiet around here—but maybe that's why.

Gene never used to give me Christmas presents; I had to make him do it. For 10 or 15 Christmases I didn't get a gift, and I just let it go. Then one year I had finally had enough. I told him, "I am not spending one more Christmas without a present. Do you understand me? I am not!" I actually stopped the car and asked him get out, go into a store, buy me something, have it wrapped, and hand it to me. I explained that this particular store was holding an estate sale and had an Edwardian cross and a ring that I really loved. "But what about the sentimental value, the feeling of being surprised," he sputtered. "Just go in and buy it," I told him; so he did. He marched in and got them. Well, he had to; I was driving and said, "I'm not taking you home until you do."

He will never forget that day, I'm sure. Later, when I received compliments on those antique pieces, Gene would say, "Oh yes, that, she made me buy it for her." And I answered, "See? Now it's sentimental. Are you happy now?

It's not that Gene is stingy—far from it; he is very generous. By the time of my Christmastime showdown, Gene had given me diamonds when my kids were born and beautiful jewelry on birthdays and other special occasions. Every piece was a special memory, something my kids had picked out or, better yet, something Gene had chosen on his own. I had my Nick diamond, my Sophie diamond, and Mother's Day gifts they had all chosen together for me. Gene preferred to buy me a present for no reason at all. One day I was surprised with a 17-karat diamond ring for no apparent reason. That was brilliant; that was wonderful, but that one year I just finally got fed up. I wanted my Christmas present at Christmastime! One December, while we were watching television, an ad for Zales Jewelers offered diamond earrings for $98. Gene remarked that I wouldn't want those particular earrings, even if I got them on Christmas Day. I told him that I would love any unprompted gift from his heart, provided it came on the right day. To his credit, he found a Zales store—his first foray into a mall—and bought back said earrings for Christmas. I cried… then I said, "Where's my real present?"

Sometimes, you just have to make them do it. And now we compromise: I won't shove the tree up his ass and he gets me a present, that's the way it works. And I would like to report that our latest Christmas was a banner year for surprises at the Tweed-Simmons household. Daddy done good!

⌣　　⌣　　⌣

I always stored my jewelry in a safe, which was normally kept in a vault in our home. The safe, which locked with a key, weighed 50 pounds and was too big for someone to carry away. I never imagined that someone would find the key, remove the jewelry from the safe, lock it up again, and return the key.

During the week between Christmas and New Year's Eve 2001 I planned to wear some jewelry for holiday parties. I immediately realized something was wrong when I saw that the key wasn't in its usual place. When I picked up the safe and shook it, I could hear the boxes with something in them rattling around, but I couldn't find the key. I had someone come to the house to drill the safe open; when I looked inside, all the boxes were empty. The thief had been smart enough to open the safe, remove the jewelry and leave the boxes inside with something in them to make the rattling sound so I wouldn't notice until I opened the safe.

I was very sad, and felt even worse for Gene. He doesn't spend his money easily; these were things that were truly an emotional sacrifice for him to buy. Buying girls diamonds? He had never done anything like that before. Now they were all gone. Gene was very calm when I told him about the theft. He said, "It's just stuff, Shannon. We'll get more. Relax."

I was crying hysterically. "It's not just stuff, it's things you gave me, jewelry my kids gave me, things that really meant something to me, and it's all gone!"

The same detective who had tested the crazy English nanny years before came back to assist in the investigation. Because we had been under construction, we had to spend one thousand dollars on each lie detector test administered to every person who had been working on our house within the previous month. Only one man became indignant about taking the test, which he didn't pass. He immediately hired a lawyer—a bad sign. Then the worker quit, another very bad sign. None of the jewelry has shown any signs of surfacing, and it's been three years now.

The results of a lie detector test are not enough evidence to search somebody's house. Not that any of the stolen items would be at his house by then anyway—that jewelry was probably well on its way to a black market where it could be sold without drawing attention. The best the police could do was to keep an eye out for the serial numbers on the stolen watches and report them to area jewelers.

Until I let go, I wanted revenge. I was furious, and I wanted whoever did this to be punished. This is another point where Gene and I differ. He didn't want to live with the thought that someone, angry that we went after him, might come after us. But Gene works so hard, and so much thought and love had gone into those gifts for me—I felt sad for that.

CHAPTER FOURTEEN

Till Death Do Us Part

Looking back has made me realize that much of what came to me was dumb luck. In many ways I feel like my life was something that happened to me. Of course I made choices and decisions along the way that led me to where I am, but so many things just seemed to fall on me. I tripped my way up the ladder; I certainly never had a master plan.

I consider myself lucky when I look at Gene—when I see him as if for the first time, or as someone else might see him. He's handsome when he gets cleaned up. I still get butterflies.

After I turned 40, work started to slow down, and I'm not anxious to do any more love scenes or B movies that take me away from my kids. I have a soccer-mom kind of life now, and I love it. I feel like I'm where I'm supposed to be all the time and doing what I was put on this earth to do, but things are changing quickly. The kids are growing up and I'm wondering what will be in store for me. I'll have to wait and see, but one thing I am very sure of is that we've brought up some fabulous human beings that will make the world a better place.

These days I get up, make breakfast, and drive the kids to school. Then I head to the gym or run errands, grocery shop, pick up the cleaning—that sort of stuff. I go back to school midday to serve hot lunch to hundreds of kids! I get to see Nick and Sophie, which I like. That means on days when I pick them up from school, I have made three round-trips. It's a lot of driving, a lot of schlepping, which means I have become addicted to audiobooks. I'm basically a shuttle driver, because the kids are still at the age where they need to be driven to all their activities. Then there are piano lessons, tutoring, riding lessons, guitar lessons, and homework. Plus I like to see my friends and other family members once in a while. My days are very full, but I can smell the day coming when I might go back to work, when the kids are grown, just to stay busy. Maybe I'll get better roles now.

I can see the moment I come into the house what Gene's been up to on any given day, because he leaves a trail of crumbs. I'll see he had a meeting here, walked over there and left a soda can, and came into the kitchen and had salad for lunch—there's some chicken left out and here's something sprayed all over the inside of the microwave. I don't know what that is. Usually something has exploded, because Gene believes that you have to cook things for an hour. He likes his food burnt to a crisp. I have to cook meat for the rest of us, then meat for him—charred to within an inch of its life, so it's unrecognizable. What starts out as a nice chicken breast

MY BEAUTIFUL CHILDREN AND OUR BELOVED DOG SNIPPET.

becomes a piece of dead black bark. Then he covers it in ketchup or salsa—everything. I did sneak some pork by him once; he liked it, until I told him it was pork.

Gene and I don't drink, and we don't even go out much anymore—maybe to a birthday party or some special event. We did attend Hugh Hefner's New Year's Eve party at the Mansion this year. I'm glad we'll always be friends, and I'm happy that Gene and Hef like each other. But that was a pretty big night out; mainly, we enjoy restaurants, movies, and comedy clubs. Gene works more now than he ever has, so sometimes he has business dinners or meetings with investors, business/social occasions he needs to attend. I don't go to many of these. He does fine without me, and I'm not the little lady who has to entertain the business clients. It's part of the deal Gene made with me, I think, for not being married: the little woman does what she pleases. And what pleases me is taking care of our kids.

RECENT HEADSHOTS FOR
WORK. MOMMY PARTS?

When I see how my life has evolved, though, it seems odd for me to be dependent on someone else financially; I'm thankful for it, but I would prefer to be working for my own money. When an acting job comes my way, I'm fortunate to have help at home so I can just take off and do it. It's almost like a vacation, to go to work; I head off and have my hair and makeup done, and someone brings me lattes and drives me around. I love that!

Friday night is our family night when we all see a movie together. On Sundays we spend the whole day together—another movie, bowling, the beach, tobogganing, whatever—just doing regular, everyday family stuff. Only now boyfriends and girlfriends are coming along with the kids.

Here we are, twenty-two years down the road, and Gene and I have a slightly different bedroom ritual than the candlelit routine we started with. When we first moved in together, and before the kids arrived, we slept naked. Now before he gets in bed, Gene puts on sweatpants and then socks, carefully tucking the sweatpants into the socks so they don't ride up. Then he puts on a T-shirt and a long-sleeved denim shirt, buttoned at the wrists so the cuffs don't ride up. Once he's all covered up, he climbs into bed and goes to sleep, bundled up like a snowman. I laugh about it every night and say, *Rock on!* to myself. Gene likes to be bundled and tucked with heavy weighted blankets. I don't know why he needs them, because within an hour of his starting to snore he kicks them off onto me. I'm

RECENT PHOTO BY RICHARD FEGELY FOR PLAYBOY.

not sure if it's my age or my hormones, but I'm already hot, so this wakes me up and just drives me nuts.

No matter how long you've known each other, there's that moment before you go to sleep when you wonder what's going to happen that night. Always be prepared is my motto—take a nice shower, try to look pretty, put a cute little nightie on—then I come to bed and he's tucking the sweats into the socks. Oh well, they can always come off! It's become a comical Archie Bunker routine. Who knows what he'll be doing the older he gets? More of those funny little things that old guys do? I'm waiting to see. And I'm sure they will seem just as adorable to me as his other eccentricities, because the man still turns my crank.

Acknowledgments

I would like to acknowledge the following people who have helped me along the way:

The Playboy team: Hugh Hefner, Dick Rosenzweig, Mary O'Connor, Marilyn Grabowski, and Joe Piastro.

At work: Andrew Stevens; Ashock Armitraj; Terry Hogan and TNT; Tom Arnold, Oliver Hudson, Michael Des Barres and the My Guide to Becoming a Rock Star family at the WB; Dierdre Hall and the Days of our Lives family at NBC; Falcon Crest and CBS; Doug Swartz, Pam Anderson and Baywatch; Leslie Greif and Adam Reed at the Greif Company; Don Carmody.

I'd also like to thank HBO and A&E, home of Gene Simmons Family Jewels.

My manager Danielle Allman and whoever becomes my new agent—I really need one!

A special thanks to all of my amazing girlfriends!

The artists: Richard Fegeley, Olivia, George Hurrell, Leroy Nieman and Patrick Nagel.

Thank you, Dr. George Weinberger, for delivering both of my beautiful children. And thank you, Dr. Frank Ryan, for the Bony Pony Ranch and Dr. Charles Rish, for looking out for my whole family.

I owe a big debt of gratitude to Tawny and Millie for practically raising my children, along with Walter Rodriguez, my second son. Thanks to Lisa Brown and Pablo for taking such good care of Sophie.

Thank you, Wildwood School, for being such a nurturing environment and positive force for so many great kids, including mine.

Tim Brennen and Terry McNamara of Action Builders; Jim Purcell; Michelle Cassio Interiors; and Stephanie Rose Landscape Design for our beautiful home.

Many thanks to Billy Blanks; Jon Jon Parks at Westside Velocity for keeping me in shape; Eric Johnson and Jerric Fruits for my beautiful hair; Tom at Rainbow Pro Nails; and Bob Harper— you go, boy!

Elanna Switzer, travel agent extraordinaire.

On this book project, publisher Michael Viner and Julie McCarron. Special thanks to Cindy Gold, who took a great cover shot, and Hugh Milstein of Digital Fusion for the retouching job.

Finally, if I'm allowed to acknowledge a place, I'd like to salute the greatly under-recognized Newfoundland, Saskatoon, Ottawa and Toronto...and L.A., of course, where my new life began.